The Politics of the New Centre

'Visions are nothing but strategies for action'

Roman Herzog
Former President of the Federal Republic of Germany

The Politics of the New Centre

Bodo Hombach

Translated by Ronald Taylor

Published in association with
The Foreign Policy Centre

Polity Press

First published in 2000 by Polity Press in association with
Blackwell Publishers Ltd

Editorial office:
Polity Press
65 Bridge Street
Cambridge CB2 1UR, UK

Marketing and production:
Blackwell Publishers Ltd
108 Cowley Road
Oxford OX4 1JF, UK

Published in the USA by
Blackwell Publishers Inc.
Commerce Place
350 Main Street
Malden, MA 02148, USA

ISBN 0-7456-2460-X
ISBN 0-7456-2461-8 (pbk)

A catalogue record for this book is available from the British Library
and has been applied for from the Library of Congress.

Typeset in 11 on 13pt Berling
by Graphicraft Limited, Hong Kong
Printed in Great Britain by T.J. International Limited, Padstow, Cornwall

This book is printed on acid-free paper.

Contents

Preface

Bodo Hombach had a major role in the reconstruction of leftist politics in Germany that led to the electoral victory of the Social Democratic Party (SPD) in 1998. The history of German social democracy over the past two decades or so quite closely resembles that of the Labour Party in Britain and it isn't surprising that the author makes considerable play with the changes initiated by New Labour in the UK.

When Labour fell into opposition in 1979 it seemed as though the party would soon return to power. In the event, Labour was out of government for eighteen years. The Social Democrats lost power in Germany in 1982. Against most people's expectations at that time they were in opposition for sixteen years. As in the UK, prominent groups within the SPD moved leftwards in the 1980s – under the influence of the 'young socialists'. The consequences for the party were disastrous. The candidate in 1990, Oskar Lafontaine, presided over a fall in the SPD vote to 33 per cent. Although the party did better in the 1994 elections, the Christian Democrats remained in power.

Under the leadership of Gerhard Schröder, the SPD made very substantial gains almost everywhere in 1998 and reassumed the reins of government. The electoral victories of the Labour Party and the German Social Democrats were not isolated events. Left-of-centre governments, or left-of-centre coalitions, have come into power not only in most of the EU countries but in many other areas of the world too. They have all done so by putting into place far-reaching ideological changes. Social democrats by and large have only been successful at the ballot box where they have been courageous enough to reject some of the tenets of traditional leftism. The issues involved here have become part of a worldwide discussion about the possibilities of 'third way' politics. The German Social Democrats by and large have shied away from using the term 'third way', preferring the 'new centre'. But, as Mark Leonard's Introduction indicates, what is at issue everywhere is the effective and progressive modernization of left-of-centre politics.

Hombach's book contains some original contributions to this debate – the book is an integral part of endeavours to rethink political philosophy and practice being made elsewhere. Different countries are coming from varying trajectories to the third way debate and with varying needs. The UK, for example, simply has too much poverty and inequality – new strategies are required to cope with the problem. Germany is more egalitarian and its needs are somewhat different. Hombach traces them to the rather fixed and static nature of the German economy and wider society. The very condition of Germany's past economic success, the 'Rhineland model of capitalism', in today's conditions is acting as a brake for further development. The model should not be jettisoned. Hombach says, but a key issue is how to 'unfreeze' German society.

The Germans have 'lost their entrepreneurial spirit'. The much-vaunted German system of industrial training has become too rigid for the needs of the new, fast-moving 'knowledge economy'. Changes need to be made in the structure of government itself and in related institutions such as the civil service. Hombach stresses that the third way project should draw upon concrete reforms being developed by social democratic parties in different contexts. We should not be concerned only with the policies of New Labour, or those initiated by the Clintonite democrats in America. The 'Polder Model' in the Netherlands is just as relevant, as is the Danish 'negotiated economy'.

The 'new centre' is more than merely a political slogan. Social democracy, Hombach shows, must respond to the profound changes that have happened in the class structure of Western countries. Traditional blue-collar manufacturing jobs have declined dramatically, while new forms of 'symbolic work' have expanded, especially those influenced by information technology.

No social democratic party can achieve more electoral support if it cannot appeal to middle-class groups as well as established left-of-centre voters. Gerhard Schröder has defined the new centre as 'people having a scientific-technical background, the cultural elite, but also small and medium-level entrepreneurs'. As in the case of New Labour, the SDP's victory was assured because the party did in fact for the first time receive significant support from such groups. Most of these voters, as Hombach shows, have not got firm party affiliations. Parties must fight for their votes rather than take them for granted.

Hombach has interesting comments to make, and policy proposals to suggest, in most of the key areas of political modernization. Welfare reform is integral to the new politics, not in order to renege on left-of-centre values, but in order to make them count in the face of major and social economic change. To remain effective, the welfare state must be restructured. Hombach is very well aware that such an objective is much easier to assert in principle than it is to achieve in practice. Any left-of-centre party that shirks the task, however, cannot hope to retain the trust of the electorate for long. Welfare reform is needed partly to respond to demographic changes, such as those producing a 'pensions crisis' due to the ageing of the population. More important, it is needed in order to cope with the problem of mass unemployment and in order to promote individual initiative and responsibility.

'No rights without responsibilities' is a basic feature of the new social contract which left-of-centre parties want to bring into being. People want to have the freedom to develop their own lives rather than being controlled by government or the state. But with such freedom and individualization must come responsibility. This does not mean, Hombach is at pains to point out, a reduced role for government, but it does suggest that that role should be reoriented. Government should look to develop a 'left supply-side polocy', based on investment in human capital and infrastructure. The active state must continue to concern itself with promoting equality. Personal initiative and social pluralism are only possible, however, where we think primarily in terms of equality of opportunity. As Hombach puts it, we should look for 'equality at the beginning' rather than 'equality at the end'. Redistribution is still necessary to achieve such an aim, but this should be redistribution in the service of opportunity.

The ideas presented here will help give form and substance
to the evolution of the debate about third way politics in the
English-speaking world. This translation of Hombach's book is a
welcome event. His work should provoke as much interest, and
controversy, as it did on its initial appearance in Germany.

Introduction

When the American magazine *Newsweek* nominated European Social Democracy as its personality of the year in December 1998, it was recognizing that the political contours of Western Europe were being rewritten. Just as the welfarist left's ideas had dominated in the immediate post-war period, and the neo-liberal right had laid claim to the 1980s and early 1990s, it seemed we were about to enter a new epoch. The greying faces of Helmut Kohl, John Major, Ruud Lubbers, Carl Bildt and Alain Juppé had been replaced by a new generation of fresh-faced '68ers hungry for power and eager to leave their mark on history. And they had begun rewriting the rules of political engagement in Europe. It was not just that social democrats were in power in thirteen out of fifteen European countries – the new governments were doing things that used to be thought contradictory: extolling free enterprise and social justice in equal measure; pledging to deliver full employment but abandoning Keynesian macro-economics; running a tight fiscal policy, but increasing investment; cutting tax at the bottom end of the labour market, but ensuring minimum standards at work; extending public/private partnership and competition but expanding and improving universal public services; devolving power and increasing local democracy, while reinventing and strengthening government at the centre to make it more efficient.

So far, there is no single guiding philosopher like Keynes or Friedman whose writings are the sacraments of this new era of politics. But there are the outlines of a new approach which

Gerhard Schröder has dubbed 'Die Neue Mitte' and Tony Blair
has called 'The Third Way', which act as a connection chain
across Europe and across the Atlantic. Bodo Hombach's best-
selling book is one of the clearest and most influential attempts
to put flesh on this new form of politics. Ranking alongside
Anthony Giddens's *The Third Way* and the Mandelson–Liddle
The Blair Revolution in the canon of modernizing social democratic texts, *The Politics of the New Centre* is a vital contribution
to European debate about the modernized left, and a key mile-
stone in the creation of a new European domestic politics of co-
operation, comparison and competition. This introduction will
seek to put die Neue Mitte in context by showing how it has
developed as a political philosophy and a political practice and
how it relates to the debate in Britain about the Third Way.[1]

Bodo Hombach, the architect of Schröder's astonishing electoral victory, was clearly seen to speak with 'his master's voice' in
this book, which marks a bold and courageous attempt to outline
a modernizing programme for the first Social Democrat (SPD)
government in over a decade. The book, like the man, is direct,
forceful and takes few prisoners – when disagreeing with the left,
it doesn't soften its blows. When Hombach is stealing his enemies'
clothes, he makes no bones about going straight for the legacy of
Ludwig Erhard, the figure who had done most to keep Social
Democrats in opposition in post-war German history. This brazen
approach is reminiscent of New Labour's attempts to capture the
mantle of Thatcherism as the radical anti-conservative force for
change. This is perhaps not surprising from a man whom Oskar
Lafontaine – the left-wing firebrand who resigned as finance minister in 1999 and who is one of Hombach's sworn enemies – has
attacked as a 'Teutonic Peter Mandelson'. But although Hombach
gets on well with Mandelson – the two men met frequently
while they were drafting the Blair–Schröder Declaration – they
are very different both in style and background. While Mandelson
is a slim, suave, aquiline figure who uses irony and wit to subtle,
but devastating, effect, Hombach is one of the biggest politicians
in German politics, physically as well as intellectually. Standing
over 6 feet tall and weighing 18 stone, he is a political bruiser
whose personal style is much closer to that of John Prescott.

The importance of Hombach's book is not just that it offers
one of the clearest and most accessible accounts of the Third

Way, or that it had a profound political impact in Germany, where it shot to the top of the best-seller list and is seen by many voters and commentators as the modernizing promise that Schröder must fulfil. It is most important because it is an attempt to show that the new modernizing social democratic governments are not just engaging in a perverse exercise of political cross-dressing, but developing a principled and practical new approach. Hombach writes of Germany 'taking its place among the reforming states of Europe which are linked by a common aim, to pursue a third way between a superficial laissez-faire liberalism and the old ideals of the Federal Republic as it developed after the Second World War'. And though he has said in many speeches that 'nothing is as convincing as actual practice', and shows contempt for social democrats who became so obsessed with theorizing that they lost their grip on reality – he is surely right that social democracy's problem has never been a shortage of political theory or vision – Hombach realizes that it is important for the centre-left to win the battle of ideas. This was brought home to me when a senior socialist politician in France told me that 'the Third Way is fine in practice, but terrible in theory'.

The problem for the Third Way/Neue Mitte is that though policy wonks, civil servants and think-tankers have rarely been so excited, it leaves large chunks of the public and the media cold. Most people have barely registered the phrase. The media see it as no more than wanting to have your cake and eat it – and are simply waiting for the inevitable contradictions to resurface. And the new political movement is not as deep in the academy as were the more tradititional forms of social democracy – so leftist intellectuals attack it for not having the sweeping scope of Keynes or Marx. Perhaps most worryingly, many party activists have not fully absorbed its meaning either – and unless this happens it is in danger of being a kitchen cabinet philosophy, rather than a kitchen table one.

Blair and Schröder are among the great communicators of our age, yet neither has entirely succeeded in making their project clearly understood to date. At the most superficial level, confusion begins with the names of the projects. It is probably too late to worry about this, but this reflects the fact that the Third Way and die Neue Mitte are part political philosophy and part political positioning – it is in the interface between the two that the potential for confusion arises. The political positioning was brilliant, from unelectability to huge popularity, from being stuck in the past to being a force for the future, but it has confused theoretical debate. The label 'Third Way/Neue Mitte' allowed both parties to break with some of the damaging, outdated and negative associations which the parties had acquired – with punitive rates of taxation, with bureaucracy and conservatism. But these labels also gave the impression that they amounted simply to value-free triangulation – famously pioneered by Dick Morris for the Clinton regime – rather than a serious attempt to modernize and update the centre-left and social democracy. That is the nature of politics where the point is to win elections rather than triumph in the seminar room. But these political realities must be borne in mind by academic scribblers and political activists who get side-tracked by manifold misinterpretations such as the notion of 'Blair as Tory', which are clearly not true, but which politicians will not dispel if they can bring in votes.

The Third Way/Neue Mitte as a Governing Philosophy

The challenge now is to flesh out the Third Way/Neue Mitte as a governing philosophy. Nobody would doubt that this is still work in progress, and there is a lot of work left to do, but to be an effective governing philosophy, a political theory needs to tell a distinctive story about the world. Marxism, conservatism, liberalism and social democracy all had four elements:

- a set of values or an underpinning ethic;
- a theory of human nature and society;
- a sense of progress and a vision of the sort of society they aimed to create;
- a road map or toolkit to guide political practice.

But the task for the twenty-first century will be for each ideological tradition to see how far its traditional answers remain relevant or credible. Hombach's book is one of the early attempts to fill in some of these gaps. So, against these criteria, how do the Third Way and die Neue Mitte measure up? And in which areas do its theorists need to develop their ideas?

Values – an ethic

The Third Way/Neue Mitte is an attempt to apply the core enlightenment values of liberty, equality and fraternity – maybe updated for modern ears as freedom, fairness and community – to the challenges which we now face. In fact, at a more fundamental level, the project has been about putting values back into politics.

For half a century, almost nobody in politics talked about values. It was not really necessary to do so. Structures were a proxy for values because the political system was stable, almost frozen. If you were in favour of more equality and improving life-chances, then in practical terms that meant supporting more redistribution through the tax structure. Those in favour of economic freedom sought to lower taxes and privatize as much as possible. Some of these traditional linkages were always a bit of a myth – and many have now been turned on their head. There can be public sector bodies which are indifferent to the public, voluntary sector organizations in fierce competition, behaving as rapaciously as any company, and large multinationals trying to cash in on the reputational advantages of being an ethical business – all of these challenge old stereotypes.

'What matters is what works' becomes the only sensible approach when means and ends become separated. This is why Hombach is not interested in structures in themselves, but in what they deliver. Hombach's and New Labour's proud pragmatism is a pragmatism of means in seeking to deliver the left's values in the most effective way today. They are dealing with changed circumstances where it has never been clearer that there are no viable alternatives to capitalism, though there may be many choices within it; where policy-makers seek to tackle multiple forms of inequality, including gender, race and social exclusion; and where citizens have very different expectations of government, and want to make choices about the decisions that affect their lives as well as the right outcomes. The world in which people were happy for the local council to choose the colour of their front doors has long disappeared – and the left has had to catch up with aspiration and ambition in order to come in from the cold. In fact, one of the most exciting things about the Third Way is that it is an attempt to settle an argument *within* the left

– between those who value individual liberty in the market economy and the commitment to social justice through collective action. Now that all thinkers and actors on the centre-left believe in market economics, these two strands of progressive thinking – social liberalism and democratic socialism – whose division for over a century has benefited only the right, can finally be brought together again.

But values, though essential, are not enough. And the centre-left today also has a better idea, and more confidence about how to put it into practice than ever before.

A theory of human nature and society

The modernizing left does have a clearer and more informed theory of human nature and society than it had in the past, or than its opponents have today. The perfectionist idea of human nature as inherently good if liberated from restraint, in either its Marxist or liberal form, has been undermined by the bloody history of the twentieth century. The reductive neo-liberal cipher of the free-standing individual, outside of all history or society, has been shown to be a dangerous myth leading to bad policy. And the right's view of humanity as fallen, as naturally wicked and needing to be restrained by authority chimes neither with our increasingly secular values, our better-educated and less deferential society, nor with our increasing knowledge of science.

The Third Way view of human nature draws upon these scientific advances, for example in the theory of evolution to reject crude social Darwinism in favour of a more nuanced theory of reciprocal altruism and enlightened self-interest which recognizes human instincts and drives both to compete and to co-operate. This leads to a politics which is optimistic but not utopian, where individual autonomy is prized and fostered but where these rights can only be understood and enjoyed in a social context which involves reciprocal duties. The communitarian approach strengthens both individual rights and healthy communities – because it understands that rights and responsibilities must go together.

This greater knowledge about the way people and societies work explains why the left has finally got markets right. We no longer regard them as inherently bad – or think that the fact that they are unplanned makes them irrational. The distortions that can appear through bureaucratic planning are well known. But the left also has a better understanding of markets than the neo-liberal right – it knows that any 'free market' exists in a social, cultural and political context and depends on social capital which the excesses of neo-liberalism diminish. The Third Way sees markets too as a means not an end – they are a good servant but a bad master. One Downing Street aide confided to me that the Third Way approach had been most elegantly and succinctly described not by Blair or Schröder, but by Lionel Jospin, the Prime Minister of France, at The Foreign Policy Centre's inaugural lecture in London, when he said 'Yes to the market economy, no to the market society'.

A vision of the good society and a sense of progress

The Third Way has more often been defined by what it is not, than by what it is. But, in fact, Third Way thinkers have mapped out a credible and distinctive centre-left vision on all of the major issues, including those such as crime, the economy, the nation and foreign policy which used to be seen as the preserve of the right. Tony Blair's famous sound-bite 'tough on crime, tough on the causes of crime' is perhaps the most well-known illustration of how the Third Way can reshape debates previously crippled by false dichotomies. The Third Way also shows how policies to strengthen the family can be combined with a commitment to women's rights, or how patriotism can be combined with a sense of identity which includes and reflects all the communities that live in our countries and which recognizes the merits of European integration. Hombach himself recently explained how the left has reclaimed nationhood:

> a homogeneous nation only exists in the conservative imagination.
> The desire for homogeneity was repeatedly used by party right-wingers for political purposes to exclude those who were different
> – from there, it was only a short path to xenophobia and narrow-minded provincialism. These are not viable future attitudes in a Germany which lies at the heart of Europe and trades with the entire world.

On foreign policy, the left has shown that it can act with strength and resolve to protect shared values – leaving a right stuck in a Cold War mindset all at sea. The modernizing left now has a natural understanding and vision of all the key issues we face – from the knowledge economy to the environment; from strengthening communities to welfare reform.

In this sense, the Third Way is about rediscovering a sense of progress. Social democracy's nature should be to modernize – to be confident with, optimistic about and ready to face the future. But Crosland was right when he wrote in *The Conservative Enemy* (1962) that the most dangerous conservation could come from within the left itself, if the left sought to preserve society rather than finding the energy to reform and change it. Tony Blair made this point himself in his 'forces of conservatism' speech at the 1999 Labour Party Conference.

After more than three decades when social change was a problem for the left, it is once again a problem for the right, which must adjust, it seems, more than at any time since it struggled to adapt to mass enfranchisement and democracy in the early years of the twentieth century. British Euro-scepticism, the German right's opposition to updating German citizenship laws, and the US Christian Coalition's rejection even of George W. Bush's 'compassionate conservatism' show that it is the right whose ideological activists seek to prevent their politicians from catching up with the voters. Hombach argues forcefully that the CDU's traditional appeal to the triumvirate of family, church and nation is not enough. This is because the left has moved beyond economic principles to see politics as a broad cultural project about creating the sort of society we want to live in. This chimes in with Crosland's thinking. He saw the goal of socialism as making Britain 'a more colourful and civilized place to live in'.

But there is at least one central issue which we have not yet resolved – and which must always be at the heart of any left project. The expansion of life-chances is a central theme for the centre-left – it links its politics of aspiration to its anti-poverty programmes. It also recognizes that there can be social exclusion at the top as well as the bottom, and that this can disrupt social cohesion. But the Third Way has not yet decided whether inequality in itself is axiomatically bad – whether the gap in itself matters, or whether an increasing gap within an increasingly fluid social order that is rising in prosperity is acceptable. This ambivalence is deep-seated. The modernizing left is beguiled with entrepreneurship, and has attached particular importance to the new breed of internet entrepreneurs who seem able to build enormous wealth – at least on paper – out of nothing. At the same time, there is a recognition that equality of opportunity and success for one generation can mean inequality of opportunity for the next. This dilemma shows that underlying the consensus on values is a fuzziness on questions of distribution. The consensus on tactics – that punitive levels of income taxation would be counter-productive both to alleviate poverty and to win elections – has hidden a disagreement of principle. And while it would be fruitless for the centre-left to tear itself apart over a question which, at present, is only relevant in the abstract, it is important that it grapples with these questions so that it has ideological bearings when there are choices to be made. It is, however, unlikely that it will resolve them until we escape the fruitless opposition between equality of opportunity (a recipe for inequality) and equality of outcome (impossible and anti-aspirational), and begin to define an egalitarian agenda in a more nuanced way that recognizes that different rules will apply to different spheres, and that the most pressing questions are access to life-chances.

A road map or toolkit for governing

In fact, it is not only on the question of equality that the Third Way/Neue Mitte could do with clearer rules. If the centre-left is going to be able to capitalize on this political and ideological ascendancy, it will need to develop a set of tests for policy decisions at all levels. This is what will ensure that it is not just Gerhard Schröder and Tony Blair, along with other leaders and small groups of elites, who can practise the politics of The Third Way or Die Neue Mitte. As Hombach writes, the pragmatism of the Third Way has been a strength. The left, used to being derided as utopian, can now show that it is as interested in practice as in theory. But the danger of this pragmatism of means is that there is no short cut to thinking about each situation as it arises. It is important that the media, the broader public – even their own supporters – can work out the rules of what may otherwise simply seem to be a strange form of political cross-dressing. David Willetts has said of his days in the Downing Street Policy Unit during the Thatcher premiership that, whenever any issue came up, they knew what Hayek would have done. They might not always have followed this approach, but it offered a clear basis for considering the issue.

Thatcherism's energy came from the fact that everybody knew what a Thatcherite was, and anybody who wanted to be a Thatcherite – a junior minister, a policy wonk, a local government leader, a party activist – knew what they needed to do or what argument to make. Its great weakness was the crudity of the tests. The modernizing centre-left needs a more nuanced set of tests which better reflect the reality of the world in which it seeks to operate. But the Third Way/Neue Mitte is not a philosophy that has been born of a single prophet handing out commandments on tablets of stone; it is a collaborative project that does not simply define practice – it emerges from practice. In fact, there is already a remarkable consistency emerging from the practice of government across Europe which could form the beginnings of a Third Way toolkit: new forms of collective action in partnership with the private and voluntary sectors; a focus on outcomes and joined-up government to solve problems from the perspective of the consumer, not the bureaucrat; modernizing democracy and participation as well as the delivery and regulation of public sevices. And everywhere, there is an emphasis on piloting schemes in different areas rather than rolling out a massive 'one-size-fits-all' solution in Napoleonic style.

Putting the Third Way/Neue Mitte into Practice

This means that there will never be a single Third Way, but many Third Ways being developed all over Europe – in the same way that there has never been a single uniform European social model. This makes the Third Way more diverse and adaptable to national circumstances than many previous political theories, which often spoke to few societies. Marxism and developmental socialism saw themselves as templates for any society – they expected traditional differences to wither away in the face of progress. Anglo-Saxon neo-liberalism had little take-up beyond Reagan and Thatcher, and disastrous consequences when pioneered in other countries such as Russia. But a political philosophy which has room for diversity can be readily adapted to local conditions. Of course, academics will always want more clarity. There is still a large 'were Thatcher's governments ever really Thatcherite?' school of thought in the academy. But for people attuned to the reality of politics, we will need to establish a different standard of proof.

The international Third Way/Neue Mitte must be about co-operating and competing to find the best solutions. In a speech to the German Parliament, Hombach said:

> Germany's states are in competition with one another over the best solutions. Our country is in competition with other countries over the best solutions. Even Europe is in competition. In the industrial sector, learning from the competition has become common practice. The best players, the best solutions and the best methods for mastering tasks at hand serve as yardsticks. This type of benchmarking should also be practised more in the political arena.

Diversity must be used to drive policy innovation – but it can only work if there are concerted attempts to create a common political space and to compare and share good practice. That is why the last section of the Blair–Schröder declaration is on 'political benchmarking in Europe'. The key challenge of the next few years will be to build up structures and institutions which create enough contact between European policy-makers and intellectuals for us to have a single European debate rather than fifteen separate national debates. This calls for a veritable 'Ideas Schengen' which will be facilitated by the New Policy Network, a new organization dedicated to spreading policy ideas around Europe which has the support of Tony Blair.

The need for diversity reflects the fact that underlying the shared values and common approach are important differences over public spending, social structure, public expectations and political and electoral systems. The thing which has led to many disagreements is not the content of specific decisions but the context in which they are taken. David Miliband has used Freud's phrase of 'the narcissism of minor differences' to explain the misunderstandings. Commentators and activists will often forget that if Tony Blair were in coalition with the Communists and Greens – as Jospin is in France – he would probably find himself more constrained. And Social Democrats in Germany are sometimes perplexed by the situation in Holland, where Wim Kok's main coalition partner is the right-wing Liberal Party. Political language differs too. While Blair is keen to talk about his affinities

with liberalism – given his values, his internationalism and the
British centre-left's disappointments in divisions in what it thought
would be its century – liberalism in France is something of the
right, and equates with 'neo-liberal' in Anglo-Saxon countries.

The country that brings differences into sharpest focus is
the USA. And it is perhaps unfortunate for the debate amongst
European social Democrats that the Third Way is often seen as
having originated with the Democratic Leadership Council's
attempts to rethink Democrat strategy and ideology in the late
1980s and early 1990s. It is not that there aren't parallels and
things that we can learn – but in practice these are often out-
weighed by some very fundamental systematic and ideological
differences. The danger is that the spectre of the USA as the
society which has been least susceptible to socialism, because its
powerful egalitarianism found other channels, means that many
Europeans regard any thinking from that quarter as inevitably
tainted. In terms of political positioning, European social democrats can, in fact, learn a lot from the process that the DLC kicked
off. They sought to understand why they were losing; and what
they needed to do to win the confidence again of the 'Reagan
Democrats', their natural supporters who had defected to the
right. And at the level of micro-politics, the debate about reinventing government has undoubtedly been influential with all progressive policy-makers who are interested in restoring faith in
government as a deliverer of social change, but realized that it
would first have 'to do less better'. The diversity of the American
system means that it will always throw up – often at the state
and local level – progressive policies from which we can learn.
But the fate of the Third Way and the ability of European social
democracy to modernize itself should never have become in-
extricably linked to Bill Clinton's ability to deliver health-care
reform through the Senate committee labyrinth or to what will
play well on crime in the mid-West.

If European progressives wished Clinton well and were sad to
see his presidency dragged to the level of soap opera and con-
fessional chat show, the peculiarities of US politics meant that he
would never be able to be a European-style modernizing social
democrat. It is not just that to be electable he had to prove that
he would not commute electrocutions in Arkansas while on the
campaign trail, but that the USA doesn't really have a government recognizable to Europeans because of the division of power

and poor levels of party cohesion. In the place of government there is a series of issue-coalitions, which must be assembled for any legislative change. This means that the most powerful man in the world is practically the weakest head of any democratic government. He has to duck and dive and triangulate to get anything through Congress – but that is a product of the American political system, not the Third Way.

Britain and Germany

The differences between Britain and Germany are small compared to those between Europe and America. But it is impossible to understand the Third Way as a political project without exploring them. The fact that two governments, elected in similar circumstances on a similar platform, should have such different fates after the general election is striking. In the UK, the Blair administration continued to break all records for mid-term popularity, while the Schröder regime limped from electoral set-back to electoral set-back. Though it was written before the general election, Hombach's book is required reading for anyone who wants to understand how this came about.

On 27 September 1998 Germany voted emphatically for change. Gerhard Schröder's decisive victory ended the sixteen-year Kohl era and was seen as a resounding endorsement of die Neue Mitte. The German government was voted out at the ballot box for the first time, not just in the Federal Republic's 50-year anniversary, as was widely remarked, but in fact for the very first time in a national German election since 1871.

The central promise was of change, of modernization, of reform. Helmut Kohl's stature on the international stage only increased the contrast with domestic stagnation. His 1990 promise of 'blooming landscapes' after unification with the east had become a bitter joke, while the stalling of tax reform and the failure to tackle unemployment contributed to a wider feeling that the CDU did not have the energy or ability to meet the reform challenges ahead. Hombach writes of the outgoing government's sense of liberation and relief at their defeat.

All of this seems eerily reminiscent of events across the channel. There is no doubt that Blair and Schröder succeeded for very similar reasons – the need for change, the bankruptcy of the government, the assurance that the alternative offered was credible, relevant and modern. Hombach is open about his admiration and debt to New Labour. The impact of Tony Blair's electoral victory remained everywhere evident in the SPD campaign eighteen months later: the Millbank-like *die kampa* election centre, the early-pledge card, and the posters on every billboard declaiming 'Innovation und Gerechtigkeit' – the same message of modernization and social justice that Tony Blair had used seventeen months earlier. To be in Germany, and to hear Schröder dedicating himself to 'Bekämpfung von Kriminalität und ihren Ursachen' – the fight against crime and its causes – was an eerie experience.

But when reporting on the election campaign for the *New Statesman*, I found that, beneath the surface of this doppelgänger campaign, there were some important differences in the two elections. Some of these were about the electoral and political system. The electoral strategy on the ground had to be different for a proportional system, with list MPs added to constituency representation. The peculiar politics of the eastern *Länder*, which are heavily over-represented in the Bundestag, and hold the key to changes of government, were also very important. But the single most important difference was in the state of the two parties themselves. And it is the difference between the modernized and united New Labour Party, and the unmodernized and fractious SPD which explains the dramatic contrast between the two parties' relative levels of popularity – as well as Hombach's own political fate.

The road to New Labour was a long one. Tony Blair was able to build on and extend a decade of modernizing party reform, under the leadership of Neil Kinnock, and the key 'One Member One Vote' reform of the Smith period. Blair used his clear election as party leader in 1994, with 57 per cent of the vote on a widened franchise, to lead an unambiguous campaign for change. He determined to rewrite Clause 4 of the party's constitution – which in theory committed the party to common ownership which it had no intention of extending. The symbolism mattered to Blair, who wanted his party to 'say what it means, and mean what it says' and to demonstrate that Labour's change was not superficial. The 3 to 1 victory on the new Clause 4 in the electoral college – with constituency parties who balloted their members finding that they voted by 9 to 1 for change – the growth in the party's membership prior to the election and the personal and party poll ratings which Blair achieved meant that he need make no concessions to those with doubts about the New Labour project in the election manifesto, which he again ensured had the overwhelming endorsement of the party membership. On entering Downing Street, Blair was able to say clearly, without dissent, 'We ran as New Labour, we will govern as New Labour.'

Hombach shows that events in Germany unfolded differently – that party modernization would have to follow once in government. Schröder did not have three years as party leader to prepare the way for a modernizing government. The SPD chairmanship did change hands in 1995, but it was Oskar Lafontaine who took over, engineering an unprecedented coup at the dramatic Mannheim Conference with his rousing appeal to the SPD's heart. It was clear from that point that the choice for Chancellor was between Lafontaine and Schröder, but the latter was only selected in March 1998. Much of the campaign strategy was already in place by that time, although there was no doubt that the SPD had chosen the much more credible salesman for this New Labour-based modernizing campaign. Had Schröder not won such a strong victory in the Lower Saxony elections, underlining the message of the polls that he was best placed to win the voters' trust, then much of the party may have preferred to ignore his claim. With Lafontaine remaining chairman and the darling of the membership, Schröder had neither the time nor the support to take on his critics in the largely unreconstructed party; instead, he had to make a deal with them. Hombach is right that this double act worked well in the shared enterprise of the election, with Schröder speaking to and winning over the voters, while Lafontaine kept the party on board.

However, this papering over the cracks was not likely to prove sustainable. Hombach's book is full of premonitions about the dangers of an unmodernized party – but of course Lafontaine's continuing role as party chair hardly made wholehearted internal reform likely. Hombach writes eloquently that 'the significance of the striking slogan of the British Labour Party during the 1997 general election "New Labour – New Britain" was not fully grasped in Germany. It signified modernization in order to govern, then government in order to modernize' – the importance of modernizing the party as a platform for modernizing the country, and for winning the trust to govern. Much of the SPD wanted to take on board the strategy and the machinery, but not the deeper message on which Labour's rehabilitation with the voters had been based. Though Hombach's book is carefully drafted to be supportive of Lafontaine and the 'two-headed' strategy, the subliminal messages are there. It was clear that the SPD could not forever delay the internal debate about which of the different analyses it favoured. An internal coalition more of convenience than conviction was going to be much harder to sustain once the imperative of winning the election was delivered, and once it faced the additional pressures of government. One can sense Hombach gearing up for this debate – while unsure about when it would begin in earnest and seeking to maintain public unity in the meantime.

Though political commentators throughout Germany and beyond never tired of pointing to the significance of this internal Schröder–Lafontaine faultline, the eruption came sooner and much more dramatically than anybody predicted. The 'Schrafontaine' phase of the SPD government came to a dramatic end when Lafontaine walked out in March 1999. It was a great surprise and did not seem to make strategic or tactical sense when 'Red Oskar' also resigned from the party and parliamentary posts which would have proved very useful in any bid for power. Some thought that Lafontaine had lost the heart for the fight – preferring political suicide, and a future as an academic and commentator, rather than a gruelling guerrilla war. But he has shown that he is as keen as ever to intervene in debate about the SPD's future. His constant sniping from the side-lines – and his viciously critical kiss-and-tell book *The Heart Beats on the Left* – have made Schröder's SPD at times look weak and divided, and made it difficult to implement the modernizing programme that the party was elected on. These acrimonious splits also explain why Schröder was forced to sacrifice his most able and trusted political lieutenant. It is true that Hombach's private affairs, dogged by controversy over the financing of his house, created ammunition for his critics, but the real reason for his premature departure from front-line politics – to run the EU's affairs in the Balkans – was that the left was keen for a scalp of its own following the loss of Lafontaine, and alleged that Hombach had undermined the Chancellor's position.

There is no doubt that these divisions have damaged the SPD's and Schröder's standing. Germany's federal system means that the electoral price of mid-term disunity can be very high. But, in many ways, Hombach's own departure from government was a pyrrhic victory for the SPD left. It was a sign that Schröder's own strategy had shifted, from encouraging 'outriders' to pursue the modernizing agenda while seeking to remain above the fray, to increasingly taking the lead himself. The July 1999 budget surprised observers with its bold moves to reform the economy. This was followed immediately by the joint launch with Tony Blair in London of *Die Neue Mitte/The Third Way* manifesto – the declaration that Hombach had drafted with Peter Mandelson. This is the most important attempt by either goverment to move forward the policy agenda for the modernizing left in power. It may also be seen as a major staging post in European political debate. It has sparked a feverish debate on the centre-left in Europe, and led to much posturing and disagreements. This is perhaps inevitable, but it marks the beginning of a genuine continent-wide debate about the future of social democracy as a modernizing force – the long-overdue moment when the battle for Europe becomes not just 'Europe less or more' or 'Europe yes or no', but actually about the values and the direction which European politics should take. There was much comment about Schröder's clear and unambiguous commitment to the moderniz-ing agenda, but it was perhaps an even more remarkable move from the British perspective. Given Britain's traditional insularity and exceptionalism, almost as much on the left as on the right, it was a major shift for the British Prime Minister to choose to share a platform with a European counterpart, to promote their shared values and agenda, rather than wrapping himself in the flag, in the days before a national election. While the document, reprinted as an appendix to this book, is debated only by the political cognoscenti in Britain, it sparked a much wider debate in Germany about the future of the SPD – both because it was Schröder's clearest declaration of the case for modernizing Ger-many and social democracy, and because the left seized upon it as a symbol of what they sought to oppose.

The internal debate within the SPD, at the time of writing, is far from settled, and it is not possible to predict confidently the immediate outcome. The SPD needs to recover its unity and sense of direction and to deliver in government if it is not to allow its opponents a good deal of short-term political capital, despite their own problems of modernizing and the party fund-ing scandal which has shaken Christian Democracy to its roots.

But the importance of Hombach's book – as both a vital contribution to and analysis of this debate – goes beyond the immediate political prospects of the Schröder government. The SPD left may have the power to block change, but the debate will be an uneven one unless they too find a way of finding a constructive, future-oriented agenda of how social democracy can adapt. At present, it is only the Third Way/Neue Mitte which offers a coherent and credible centre-left alternative. There seems little prospect at present of the SPD left, even if they were to stall or even to win the battle within the party, going on to win elections against the CDU by presenting a compelling and popular analysis which strikes a chord with German voters as well as activists.

Hombach's book explains very clearly why economic, social and political change make modernization an imperative, which offers the centre-left a golden opportunity at last to put its values into practice. The threat to the ideological and electoral ascendency of modernized social democrats will not come primarily from parties of the right – their political programmes and values seem disconnected from an increasingly interdependent world. But the left can damage and marginalize itself once again if it cannot overcome its own often deeply ingrained conservatism. To fight tooth and nail against the reforming project would be needlessly to throw away the opportunity to define a whole generation of politics in Europe. And it would be likely to bring nothing better than defeat, the soul-searching of hundreds more 'What's Left?' seminars so familiar to both Labour and SPD supporters in the wilderness years of opposition.

And it would become clear that a modernizing project like Hombach's would again be the only way back – the clear alternative to the decline into irrelevance in the face of seemingly inexorable social change, such as that experienced, for example, by French Marxism, which was so strong just a generation ago. The left can be of the future or it can be defeated by it. The choice will again be to modernize and to catch up, or to wither away. The SPD should have learnt enough from its own experience – never mind that accumulated by its sister parties – of the unpalatable alternative of impotent, if occasionally heart-warming, opposition to make the right choice. The challenge is to join the German voters who embraced Schröder and Hombach's Neue Mitte enthusiastically – and to join the modernizing left parties and governments of Europe in shaping the new wave of progressive politics.

Note

1 I am indebted to many people who have taken part in conversations, seminars and discussions with me about the Third Way/die Neue Mitte; in particular Bernd Becker, Heinz-Albert Huthmacher, Ernst Luebkemeier and Thomas Meyer in Germany, and Andrew Hood, Sunder Katwala, Dennis Maschane and David Miliband in Britain. I also draw on key articles, speeches, pamphlets and books, including: 'The Third Way', speech by David Miliband to the 1999 Konigswinter Conference; *The Third Way*, by Tony Blair (Fabian Society, 1998); *The Third Way*, by Anthony Giddens (Polity, 1998); *Tomorrow's Politics: the Third Way and Beyond* (Demos, 1998); *Innovation und Gerechtigkeit* (SPD, 1998); *The Federal Republic of Germany at 50* (Macmillan, 1999); *Le Manifeste Blair–Schroeder*, by Laurent Bouvet and Frederic Michel (Fondation Jean Jaures); *The Foreign Policy Centre's Inaugural Lecture*, by Lionel Jospin (www.fpc.org.uk); and *Crosland and New Labour*, by Dick Leonard (Macmillan, 1999).

Foreword to the Original German Edition

Power has changed hands in Germany. The world's press can scarcely contain itself. Superlatives abound. 'The Dawn of a New Era', we read – and that is one of the more restrained headlines.

In Germany itself the atmosphere is quieter, like being at the eye of the storm. The transfer of power has taken place without bitterness on the one side and without triumphalism on the other. The coalition of Christian Democrats and Liberals displays a strange sense of relief, of liberation – not a word about wanting to continue in office. Power was handed over in haste, as though there was no time to be lost in getting rid of the keys to the Chancellery and the ministerial offices. It slowly becomes clear how helpless and resigned the outgoing government had felt in the face of the backlog of problems and reforms which they had been unable to tackle. Decisions had been deferred, budget deficits concealed and the real facts of the situation swept under the carpet. The old coalition was more jaded than anyone was prepared to admit.

The simplistic explanation that in the last analysis the Christian Democrats (CDU) had lost the election because they had not been able to bridge the generation gap tells only half the story. In reality the coalition had become bogged down in an uncritical devotion to a free market economy whose only tools were privatization and deregulation on the one hand and a tradition-centred conservatism on the other, which set its face against any attempt at change, though sensing that disaster was just round the corner.

The CDU–Liberal coalition experimented with a variety of new strategies but could not make any of them appear credible. First, they put themselves forward as a force for continuity in an uncertain and unstable age. German reunification and the euro, the abolition of the German mark and with it the surrender of the old German identity – such were issues they could use to make people uneasy at the prospect of too much change.

Wolfgang Schäuble, then Minister of the Interior, took a different line. Acting as though the CDU had not been in power for the past sixteen years, he made out that the party was about to preside over a policy of radical change – a policy stifled at birth by the opposition of the Christian Social Union (CSU), the CDU's partners in government. Before the election, and even after it, Chancellor Kohl had repeatedly maintained that the world did not wish to see change in Germany. But the world's most influential statesmen made it clear that they were not prepared to be dictated to, and went out of their way to meet Schröder and invite him to visit their countries, even before the election. The world was left with a strange mixture of 'more of the same' – a defiant defence of the status quo – and rhetorical pledges of modernization: on the one hand a strident party political campaign, on the other an arrogant claim to being all-powerful. It was made to sound almost like a law of nature that Helmut Kohl must continue in office.

With the general election of 1998 the curtain went up on a new drama which had long been in preparation behind the scenes. The appeal to a 'New Centre' in society proved a success. Self-employed and company directors, workers – men and women alike – even from the heartlands of the CDU, all deserted the conservatives, putting their trust in a Social Democratic party whose modernizing programmes, pragmatism and sense of reality met with broad approval. Whereas the CDU/CSU, the Free Democrats (FDP) and even the Greens waged electoral campaigns addressed to their own supporters – and therefore won over hardly a single voter from another party – the politics of the 'New Centre' captured and retained the floating voters and the 'don't knows'. Instead of a protest vote, they registered a vote for rational policies. The nightmare scenario painted by the conservatives frightened no one, and the extreme right was put in its place.

The German Federal Republic has taken its place among the reforming states of Europe, which are linked by a common aim,

namely, to pursue a third way between a superficial laissez-faire
liberalism and the old ideals of the Federal Republic as it developed
after the Second World War. The coming millennium, which
Germany will enter with a new government, will witness the
historical union of true liberalism – which has in practice been
abandoned by the FDP – and the values of social democracy.
This union has already begun to dominate the political agenda,
from the left to the right.

For many this is confusing. How, they ask, can one be on the
left and at the same time negotiate in a new coalition with industry? How can one support the welfare state while also demand-
ing more responsibility on the part of the individual? How can
one advocate more competition yet at the same time offer the
individual new safeguards?

I find no ground for confusion here. We can give our traditional basic values a new significance so as to make them mean-
ingful to those who have hitherto not been on our side but have
now given us their vote of confidence. For what does justice
mean to a young apprentice who has to put in several hours'
work in order to be able to afford the theoretical equivalent of
just one of his own hours? What do the concepts of co-operation
and solidarity mean to a man starting up a new business if he has
to apply to one bank after another and still does not get the loan
he needs to embark on his venture? We live in a world in which
ideals are important but in which it is fatal to cling to ideologies.

The sociologist Richard Sennett put it thus: 'An idea must
be able to stand the test of concrete experience, otherwise it
becomes a mere abstraction.' Sound practical politics are required,
with a properly functioning political 'product' – this, after all, is
what people are paying for. They are looking to their government not for dogma but for a fundamental grasp of the realities
of the situation in which they live. The state must do its best to
assess the risk factor for the individual as far as it can. We cannot
bring the processes of economic and social change completely
under control, but we can make it possible for the individual to
deal with the challenges that confront him.

Now that the equilibrium sustained by competing systems has
been broken, the crisis facing both the traditional left and right
has become clear. In the 1980s and the first half of the 1990s the
country was presented with a false antithesis – a philosophy of
all-consuming economic growth or a hidebound defence of every

aspect of the traditional welfare state. There is no way back to redistributive policies. The renewal of the social democratic model that supersedes the categories of 'left' and 'right' is an international model. There are still murmurings of discontent in Germany when responsibility is transferred from the state to the individual – a kind of protectionist, 'safety first' mentality. Instead of this, there must be a system of social security in place which encourages people to take risks and show flexible attitudes to change. We need equality of opportunity, equality at the outset, not at the outcome – a policy of second chances. The state must play an proactive role. We must invest in policies that promote self-help, initiative and an enterprise culture. The nation will develop a sense of common purpose only as long as the state remains proactive.

The old saw 'Carry on as before', which for years diverted people's attention from the changes that were needed, has left a heavy burden. The backlog of necessary political and social reforms has assumed massive proportions, and there is need for radical change in many areas. The principle at the heart of the welfare state is consensus, but the state's declarations of cast-iron guarantees and safeguards have increasingly become mere empty promises.

But while the need for control and a firm sense of direction grew during the Kohl era, the curtain fell on the exercise of creative government. Discussions became bogged down in squabbles about the levy to help finance German reunification, or about the reform of German spelling, which produced a vicious circle of apocalyptic vision followed by a chronic inability to engage in structural reform. There developed an inward-looking society characterized by a schism between public debate, in which all manner of illusions could be peddled with impunity, and private conversations in which people complained to each other about the real state of affairs – the future of retirement pensions, the state of the universities, tax reform and so on. Discussions were conducted not in terms of what was sensible or stupid but of what was good or bad. We live in a stagnant society, people said, whose old routines and structures were no longer capable of handling the processes of rapid change.

Reasonable and practicable proposals fell victim to the dogmatic debate over the preservation of the status quo, were tossed to and fro in endless committees, then finally forgotten. But today the process of globalization is relentlessly putting all national

social and political institutions to the test of whether they can
survive in the world of international competition. New questions
are being asked about the solidarity and cohesion of society and
about its ability to combine social security with economic efficiency. To draw the conclusion that globalization spells the
end of politics and the state and allows no scope for manoeuvre,
cannot be the last word. We can make our own decision on
whether we want to be the hammer or the anvil.

The same applies to the risks and opportunities involved in
European integration. The SPD is now facing the huge task of
helping to make economic and currency union a success. We
must make the euro an honest currency. Europe is not the prize
for our history but an opportunity for the future. But the euro
will not automatically solve our employment problems. The
innovations for which small and medium-sized businesses in
particular are looking constitute a central political issue, for a
state of continued high unemployment in Germany would pose a
serious threat to the stability of a common currency. There is
only one way to grasp the opportunities offered by such a currency, namely by creating a liberal, democratic, federal structure
which will combine the various cultural, linguistic and ethnic
traditions with the basic elements of European political unity.

Federalism, too, is what one chooses to make it. Can we live
with a federal system that does not regard equality of living
standards as an overriding necessity but is instead guided by the
principle of competition to find the best solutions? It is my conviction that the processes and institutions that are still acting as
obstructions to social and political progress must be reorganized
and rejuvenated. We have undertaken to show that there *is* an
alternative course, and the SPD must open its doors to all those
who accept the principle that 'small actions are better than big
words'. It is not a matter of good intentions – it is a question of
good results. To defend the welfare state as it stands to the
bitter end is in reality to sign its death warrant.

We are facing the most predictable and predicted crisis of the
twentieth century. For twenty years the demographic pattern has
been there for all to see, and the crisis facing the working population has been a subject for discussion since the beginning of the
1980s. But whereas in the Netherlands and elsewhere reformat-
ory measures have already been put in train, in Germany we
are still debating the issues. We are living in a negative-minded

society which has adopted the practice of putting as many obstacles as possible in other people's way, with the result that in the end no one is capable of finding an answer.

We need to get back to the principles of a social market economy. It is the declining confidence in the ability of the German political system to solve the problems facing it, not doubts about the validity of the model itself, that characterizes the crisis of identity facing the social market economy. The ideals championed by Ludwig Erhard in the 1950s are experiencing a boom, whilst at the same time confidence that the government has the ability to pave the way for the fulfilment of these ideals is shrinking. A poll revealed that 50 per cent of those aged between 14 and 29 would prefer to be self-employed. At the same time almost half were convinced that success did not depend on hard work.

The social component of the economic system is not that of the state as the confident provider of universal benefits. Rather, it presupposes that individual achievement will be rewarded with prosperity, qualification with promotion, willingness to assume responsibility with a greater scope for enterprise and initiative, and independence with the guarantee of a second chance. Erhard, Economics Minister in Adenauer's CDU government, had no thought of bequeathing his ideas to the Social Democrats. But we need to have recourse to his values of pragmatism and anti-*dirigisme* if we are to create an effective synthesis of liberal principles and the basic values of the SPD. And at the heart of this synthesis lies the reconstruction of the social market economy.

The Social Democrats have now been entrusted with fulfilling what they promised, namely to revive the economy in order to provide a basis for social and ecological reforms and for creating new jobs. Our principles are innovation and social justice – an alliance in which a modern economic policy will be combined with measures for growth and the creation of new sources of employment. We pledge that the pensions and welfare system will remain in place and be made financially viable. The older generation built up this country – now that generation is entitled to fair and guaranteed provision for its retirement. The welfare system must offer fairness and security to all those who need the support of the community.

One of the preconditions of proactive government is a greater transparency in the administration of the country's finances and of the social security budget, together with greater scope for private provision for one's own future. The system as it appears today seems to allow little scope to individual responsibility and the active co-operation of employees, whose participation is only welcomed in the form of their national insurance deductions. The severest test of our credibility, however, lies in the field of taxation policy.

The legitimacy of any taxation system depends on the clarity and transparency of its rules and the ways in which the taxes are spent. The essential features of any reform that acknowledges this are not really a subject of controversy, so now is more than ever the moment to venture along a new path. Once the principle of 'governing by taxes' has been abandoned, the way will be free for tax reductions across the board.

All such challenges have to be taken up in a spirit of co-operation, through a series of concerted actions especially at regional level. There is a new political ethos at work in German corporate culture. More open forms of negotiation and co-operation are taking shape, replacing the traditional rituals; this can be seen in a new flexibility in regional employment contracts and company agreements guaranteeing security of employment. Nor does this come a moment too soon. The years 1996 and 1997 were characterized by the abandonment of consensus and co-operation. Rhineland capitalism, the model of an institutionalized balance of interests between state, employers and the workforce, has in recent years come to be dismissed as a fudge, and it is alarming to what extent we have found ourselves drifting away from constructive attitudes.

In the *Land* of North-Rhine-Westphalia we have been testing out a new concept known as 'creative corporatism', where politicians sit down with the representatives of industry, works councils and trade unions who have a will to tackle specific problems – men and women who are not necessarily those in official positions. Top officials on both sides have had their problems with this approach. But pragmatic consensus is at the heart of the social market economy. All European countries which have a positive balance of employment have voted to adopt such triple alliances between government, unions and employers as a way to combat unemployment and reform the employment market and the welfare state. The only alternative to consensus is stagnation. Having formed a new alliance, we must put all these interlocking subjects on to a common agenda of co-operative economic policies. And the more comprehensive the total package, the easier agreement on common goals will be to reach.

There is a need, particularly in economic policy, for more radicalism in dealing with practical issues. For too long we have been stuck in a groove arguing about supply-side policies and demand-side policies. Most people have long abandoned the once-praised panaceas associated with the policies of John Maynard Keynes. Innovative industries and people setting up new businesses need a totally new kind of economic policy. Subsidies will be given to companies that come up with the best proposals. Without a change in our attitude towards competition and business risk, any effort to reform our economy will be doomed to failure. What we need is a 'left-wing supply-side policy', a modern enterprise economy aimed at improving overall economic conditions and combining dynamism with a coherent employment policy. The costs of the inevitable frictions and teething troubles that will accompany the introduction of the new system will have to be met from the public purse. In such a situation the attitude to innovation is far more important for a locality than matters of cost. If, as a result of a particular infrastructure, a region proves a particular expertise in an innovative field, research grants and production investments will flood in from all over the world, showing that globalization and regionalization can go hand in hand. A central requirement here is for closer links between science and industry. Industry needs to know what science can achieve, and science must listen to the needs of industry.

This would also be a model for the modernization of our universities and technical colleges. We are confronting changes in the German university system comparable to those which took place with the reforms of the 1960s and 1970s, and which will lead to much greater competition. The scope for innovation and expansion in the industries of the future depends on the availability of qualified men and women – in some sectors, indeed, a lack of young recruits is already putting a brake on development. The whole system of future education and training is in urgent need of overhaul. The comprehensive plan put forward by the *Land* of North-Rhine-Westphalia shows how the problem could be approached.

Another plan is for a sound basic training followed by regular re-qualification and opportunities for further training. My vision is of a society in which there are no longer periods of unemployment but only periods of re-training or re-learning – unemployment seen as preparation for entering a new field of activity. We need a new concept of education. We are highly qualified but are slow to diversify, and we carry with us a stock of superfluous knowledge. This shows how comprehensive my concept of change needs to be. The ability to innovate is a matter for the whole of society, one that affects mentalities and infrastructures in government, administration, schools, science and our whole pattern of training. We must replace anxiety about the future and the fear of risk with knowledge and confidence in dealing with new and risk-bearing technologies. The greatest opportunities lie with technological innovations which can help to solve social problems.

New jobs will only come with the establishment of new companies. In North-Rhine-Westphalia, starting in 1996, we have been spending between 300 and 400 million marks a year on helping to finance the setting up of new companies under the scheme 'Go!'. This is a project that promotes a culture of independence and a social climate favourable to the foundation of new businesses. In addition we require a fundamentally new culture for capital provision – it must again be made profitable to invest in factories and jobs instead of in empty buildings. How important it is for the employment situation that independent entrepreneurs are prepared to invest can be seen from the statistics. In the coming years almost 80,000 middle-ranking employers and tradesmen in North-Rhine-Westphalia alone will take up retirement. For 20,000 of these there is nobody to take their place, putting at least 200,000 jobs at risk. In certain selected areas, therefore, those looking to set up new businesses are being put in touch with entrepreneurs who are looking for successors in their own companies. In such alliances the state must demonstrate that it is capable of matching or even surpassing what it demands of others. We need to take a fresh look at the functions of the state. The state is not so much a producer as a sponsor, an encourager, an active partner. Anyone who has cause to deal with the organs of the state must be given help to embark on new initiatives, show commitment, make investments, take on responsibilities. Government departments must be there to help, not to hinder.

Our policies must strike a new balance between guaranteed rights and positive obligations. The policy of making cuts in areas

where the least opposition was to be expected has only intensified the crisis of identity in the welfare state over recent years.
Every programme and every institution must be subjected to the
same question – are we really getting for our money what we are
entitled to expect? The basic principle of our policy is fairness –
fairness for those who need help but also for those who provide
that help. The financial crisis in the redistributive state offers at
the same time a great opportunity to the proactive welfare state.
Why should it be regarded as more socially responsible to relieve
people of their responsibilities than to help them to assume responsibility on their own account? By distributing resources rather
than opportunities the welfare state is following a collision course.
We must change the welfare state from being a safety net into
becoming a trampoline. Or, to change the metaphor, it must
stop being a hammock and become a springboard that catapults
the individual back into active working life, restoring his sense of
responsibility and giving him a stake in society.

State intervention is only justified if it encourages the individual's abilities and challenges his sense of initiative and does
not merely offer him some kind of material assistance. Everywhere
in Europe traditional conceptions of work are undergoing radical
change. 'Any job is better than none', is the new motto. Work,
even in low-paid, menial jobs, contributes more to the individual's
self-esteem than any welfare hand-out, however generous. The vital
question is whether we can combine social security and job promotion in such a way that more jobs are created and at the same
time there are greater incentives to take them up. Hitherto, all
attempts at introducing a 'joint wage' of this kind have ended in
failure. But social security distorts the labour market at the bottom end, therefore it would be sensible to experiment in certain
regions or certain industries with such measures as subsidization
of the employer's wage-added costs in the case of low-skill workers.

A further example of how previous assumptions about the
welfare state are changing is that of compulsory pensions insurance. The pension debate of recent years, coupled with the assurance given by the CDU minister Norbert Blüm that 'pensions are
safe', has totally unsettled the electorate. Every attempt at reform
was branded as an attack on the so-called 'generation contract',
and to draw a comparison between the financial return on the
state pension fund and that on Stock Exchange investment was
taboo.

Kurt Biedenkopf, for example, Prime Minister of the *Land* of
Saxony, put forward proposals for a basic pension which would
have been totally unworkable but which at the same time drew
attention to the real issues. Who can accept a system in which
the average worker pays 20 per cent of his wages towards his
retirement pension, when one in four will only get back a pension at the basic welfare level?

The most serious consequences for our contributions-based
pensions system flow from the situation in the labour market,
where the proportion of workers in full-time employment is
shrinking, while that of those in temporary, part-time or casual
employment is constantly growing. A guarantee of one's status
after retirement is proving increasingly difficult to deliver on the
basis of the national retirement scheme alone. In the first instance,
therefore, we need a firmly established system which provides
security in three respects – a guaranteed pension for those in
retirement, the entitlement of workers to the benefits to which
they have contributed, but also a pledge to young people that,
after a transitional period, they too will receive an adequate pension in retirement. Figures show that today around 80 per cent
of the working population are prepared to make their own provision for retirement. But many households, caught between
declining real incomes and increases in welfare contributions,
find themselves unable to do much about the situation.

If we are to persuade the citizens of this country to join us in
the search for a co-operative system of social security, we must
have the courage to make a thorough examination of our finances.
Hiding the real problems only has the result of making the whole
question of social security an irritating issue which lies beyond
the bounds of reform, driving more and more people to take
refuge in the grey economy. We need a number of things: a
guaranteed retirement pension that will provide a calculable sum
in old age; a second source of capital reserves; a general overhaul of
company pensions; and a more active participation by employees
in the creation of economic wealth.

Any fundamental reform must avoid over-taxing the 25–45
age group during the transition period. But the transition to
such a scheme *is* possible – though it becomes year by year more
difficult. A period of less than thirty years would be unrealistic,
but if we had made a start fifteen years ago, when the forecasts
were already available, we would by now have been halfway

towards our goal. The younger generation do not wish to withdraw from the 'generation contract', but at the same time they want to know what it implies – clear obligations in return for new guarantees.

This could be the starting-point for a new social contract. Our policies must do everything possible to improve the opportunities available to those who create the wealth in society which is necessary to finance the welfare state. It is far more important to get rid of the fossilized features of our educational system, to make our universities and polytechnics centres for founding new businesses and to promote innovation, than to indulge in discussions over statistics and the technical details of insurance.

Following the Bundestag election of 1998 the Social Democrats have found themselves facing demands for modern, pragmatic policies that leave no room for the old ideological attitudes. This is both a great opportunity and a great challenge. But the end of the century finds the other parties facing a crisis. On the one hand the Greens will have to make a painful decision between fundamentalism and the demands of *realpolitik*, while the Christian Democrats find themselves torn between the last idealistic remnants of old-style conservatism and a free market economy which no longer has any use for such a philosophy. The SPD is part of a coalition – a coalition of modernizers that must dispense with ideology, otherwise it will fail. It has regained control of the social agenda. At the end of the 1980s there were a few in the ranks of the SPD itself who seemed to give the impression that the pace of progress was being dictated by the Greens, who had somehow already reached a position to which the Social Democrats themselves aspired. Since then, however, Gerhard Schröder has made the SPD into a strong and confident party which has picked up the reins of leadership, sure in the knowledge that it has the best policies for dealing with the problems that face us – in particular, the conception of economic success as the foundation for social and ecological modernization.

This book is both a challenge and an appeal to all who have the will and the capacity to join with us in undertaking this task of reform. It is a plea for a new awakening, for a policy of the 'New Centre', the middle ground that voted for us in the general election. We appeal to the occupants of this middle ground to join an alliance pledged to change – men and women who want practical solutions, are undogmatic and free from ideology, and are looking for political leadership. The Social Democrats must strive with might and main to consolidate and expand their influence in this new middle ground. This is the only way that reforms can be brought about and the majority of the electorate be won over to policies of radical and long-lasting change.

We must use the hope for a modernization of society that was linked with the victory of the SPD in the 1998 election to undertake a fundamental reform of the party. I have therefore drawn particular attention in this book to the structural problems facing German political parties. The significance of the striking slogan of the British Labour Party during the 1997 general election, 'New Labour – New Britain', was not fully grasped in Germany. It signified modernization in order to govern, then government in order to modernize. People who still stand 100 per cent behind every party resolution and support every detail of the party programme have lost touch with reality.

Most people take a more sober view – sometimes one party is right, sometimes another; on occasion one party may be regarded as more right than another. Those in positions of responsibility in the economic and cultural life of the country are scared off by the party political system. Yet I cannot conceive of solutions to the urgent problems that will confront us in the future without the parties. Somehow they must regain control of the agenda of the large-scale issues that face the country.

It is a paradoxical situation. The parties and the corporate sector are the only organizations that can break the log-jam. But at the same time it is they that are responsible for the log-jam in the first place. The electorate look to their politicians to intervene not less often but with a greater sense of purpose and determination. As New Labour in Britain and the Democratic Party in America have discovered, success attends workable policies. Labour's courage to tackle controversial issues should help the cause of the Social Democrats. Structural changes are being demanded of the SPD since the election which are bound to lead to controversy both inside and outside the party. The key point is that Tony Blair and New Labour have always combined cuts and the need for sacrifice with a guarantee of new safeguards. This is the source of the support which the British Labour government continues to enjoy, a support based on the slogan 'To govern for the many, not the few'.

We Social Democrats are in a privileged position. Whereas we used to be criticized for too much theorizing and for having too many illusions and utopian visions in our programmes, today we are in the happy position of being able to point to a number of European states in which such reforms have been successfully carried through. Social democratic parties in these countries have shown how the state can promote innovation in society and in the economy, cut unemployment and at the same time put a stop to escalating national debts. Taking such success stories as a benchmark makes it easier for us to find our own solutions. And the more examples we find, the more readily these solutions will be accepted. In the past the SPD's debates on reform did not cast their net widely enough and ignored a mass of relevant experience from without. In selecting from among the many available options for discussion, I have therefore laid special emphasis on international comparisons. Such comparisons must become a central feature of all debates on reform in Europe. I could even envisage an international competition for the best projects in which everybody could learn from the most successful proposals.

At first sight, the mountain of necessary reforms is so huge that one is tempted to throw up one's hands in despair. But on a closer and more systematic view it can be seen how closely interwoven the various fields are. It becomes apparent, for example, that the burden of wage-added costs is distorting the labour market, blocking investment and creating new injustices. The familiar basic principles of social security often turn out to be a trap, when what is at stake is to reward individual initiative and independence. It is therefore not without reason that ideas discussed in one chapter of this book should later reappear in another. This is the only way, in my view, that the reader, especially one who does not choose to read the book from cover to cover at a single sitting, will be able to see the context clearly.

It is a German weakness to study charts of economic performance, hope for a miraculous improvement in the economic situation and, with every upturn, put off making necessary changes. The boom at the time of reunification revealed this clearly. This is surely the moment when we must achieve the social breakthrough – not by rolling back the state but by escaping from the grip of a belief that there is no alternative, by concluding a new social contract with a proactive entrepreneurial state, by reassessing

the balance between rights and obligations, by being prepared
to take risks in a climate where talk is more of the opportunities
offered by change than of its dangers.

Willy Brandt once said: 'The man who seeks to preserve what
is worth preserving must change what needs changing.' Confidence in the future means taking risks. To avoid taking risks is
to take the greatest risk of all. We must abandon the stance of
anxious spectators. And not just politicians – but all of us.

Bodo Hombach

1

Breaking the Mould

The Social Democrats have a programme that they propose as an alternative to neo-liberalism – a pragmatic programme that takes account of practical realities, while acknowledging the necessity of dispensing with the ideologies of property rights and redistributive economics but only in combination with new safeguards. We are all facing the challenge to create a new model for Germany, a policy that will steer a third course, a path between competing ideologies, a system that represents a realistic response to the changes that have taken place in the world. We are facing the decision of whether we wish to become pioneers of a politics of the 'New Centre', superseding the extremes of free market economics on the one hand and a centralized welfare state economy on the other. The state is not there to offer a refuge from impending dangers, and it can do more than just preside over a process of decline. It can build bridges, not merely provide crutches for those who would otherwise be left out in the cold. Economic success and social justice are not mutually exclusive but complement each other. The sociologist Ralf Dahrendorf coined the term 'globalization plus' – a project not driven by coercion born of fear but inspired by concrete goals. In the face of institutionalized mass unemployment, the desperate financial problems endemic in the social security system, clear signs of social disintegration and of a growing inability on the part of the public to comprehend a policy based on a reluctance to resort to active intervention – in the face of all these things we can do nothing but seek to combine vision with pragmatism. Both these are at present in short supply. What we therefore need is a return to a politics based on the demonstration of reasons rather than on obsolete convictions and ideologies.

At the Social Democrats' party congress in 1973 Willy Brandt said that whoever set out in a democracy to gain a majority and exercise power must win the middle ground and hold it. The SPD was never better at doing this than in the years when it was the party of the future, the years when it had confidence in the nation without making excessive demands on it. For how can people have confidence in politics unless politics has confidence in people? We are therefore setting out to conclude a new social contract with those citizens, men and women, who occupy what we call the 'New Centre Ground' in society.

These men and women, irrespective of any socio-political criteria, share certain expectations of politics. Most belong to the 60 per cent of undecided middle-class voters not attached to any particular ideology or any particular social or political organization. They are practically-minded and undogmatic and look for down-to-earth solutions to problems and for political leadership – not politics on the grand scale but pragmatic and properly thought out. They have turned their backs on the political parties and the state because they expected initiatives from the government that have not been fulfilled. They have no wish to be tied into a comprehensive system of state benefits at all costs, nor do they want to be showered with grants and allowances in the name of social security. But nor do they want to risk having to give up their economic independence at the first signs of liquidity problems or being marginalized by new forms of work such as bogus self-employment.

A fundamentally new policy also requires courage, determination, persistence and a readiness to give up acquired privileges. It demands an immense degree of pragmatism on the part of all those involved. We need new models and clearly defined reform programmes to stimulate this pragmatism, this passionate desire to find practical solutions to our problems. For too long debates on restricting the power of the state and the redistribution of responsibility had a quality of insubstantiality and triviality about them, whether it was a matter of the reform of the social security system or a discussion of subsidies. Our policies can no longer be based on misleading guarantees of social security. There is consensus on the principle of the welfare state, but the notion that it will go on functioning for ever, and that it will offer a legal entitlement to care and support from the cradle to the grave, are increasingly becoming mere empty promises, trumpeted by those who, with their privileged access to inside information, ought to know better. A contract between the power of economic achievement and the welfare state, 'Rhineland capitalism' and the social market economy, a synthesis of the economy and the labour market – this is what we promise, and the social contract we offer. Our task is to produce a modernized version of this contract based on new, clearly formulated principles closely linked to the changed situation in which we now live. Employment and social justice are our twin concerns – but as they apply to a changed world. The time for patching up the status quo has passed. The need today is for a complete overhaul.

Globalization, the European economic and currency union, added to changes in society itself – the increasing proportion of retired people, the problems raised by the structurally embedded force of mass unemployment, by new patterns of productive employment and by changes in perceived values – all this raises vital questions about the nature of our society and our political institutions. By the same token there arises a need for new points of reference, a new sense of direction. We are facing a huge task. The forces that have paralysed German politics and German society over the past decade and a half, preventing them from adapting to the needs of the moment, cannot be got rid of in a few moments and with the help of a few minor reforms here and there. Their roots lie far deeper, embedded in long-established mind-sets. By challenging this situation, one is challenging the entire image that conservative-minded politicians have of man and society – not excluding politicians in the SPD itself.

The most striking feature of the German reaction to the world of the 1990s was its violent swings from euphoria to despair – an extremism often regarded by the outside world as typically German. In the early 1990s we were living in an illusion of self-satisfaction, as though we had achieved all there was to achieve and as though we needed only to bend our efforts towards preserving the present and thereby guaranteeing the future. Towards the end of the decade, however, many are preaching a gospel of gloom and doom because the reforms to the existing system appear too little, too late, leaving demands for a total reconstruction.

At the top of the list of best-selling books in 1997 was *Crash!*
by the television journalist Jürgen Roth, whose diagnosis proph-
esied a return to the class struggle:

> The walls of the houses are damp, the wallpaper is covered in
> mildew, cockroaches are crawling all over the tiny kitchen and the
> children's faces are ashen. In contrast the exterior of the hovel in
> which Frau S. has been living for five years glistens with fresh
> paint. Slowly but surely the ghost of poverty is stripping our
> society of its veneer of genteel prosperity and its respectability is
> turning out to be like the make-up a prostitute puts on her face.

Tendentious works such as *Crash!* present Germany as an under-
developed country, socially, emotionally and politically.

One consequence of this situation has been that more young
people have been emigrating from Germany than at any time in
the past. More than 900,000 left the country between 1989
and 1996 – more than in the whole of the 1950s. For 1997 the
government expected more than 350,000 to register their intention
to emigrate, with even more to come. The numbers would be
still higher if other countries had more liberal immigration policies.

The young people among these would-be emigrants give as
their main reason the 'dead weight' that has settled over Germany. What truth is there in this? As far as the politics of the
Kohl era are concerned, the curtain fell not with the failed attempt at a reform of the tax system in 1997, but earlier, in the
first half of the 1990s, when the government wasted its energies
in squabbles over the 'Reunification Levy' or the spelling reform,
an example of an obsession with a desire for regulation which
had not the slightest thing to do with such matters as the health
of the nation's society and economy. While political commentators were filling the pages of their papers with lamentations and
self-reproaches, avoiding any attempt to link the changes taking
place with the prospect of new opportunities, a scenario of decline
and fall was being painted.

But feeling oneself under threat only makes one hold on to
familiar ideas the more tightly. There arose a vicious circle of
apocalyptic world vision and psychological and structural inability to reform. It was a case of each man for himself, and the
sense of community decayed. Fear of the economic situation, the
globalization trap, the end of prosperity – doom scenarios paralysed the body politic and the body public. If a family gets stuck

in a traffic jam when going on holiday or returning home, they at least know where they are going and where they will eventually arrive. But for almost two decades all those urging political change of one kind or another have had nothing to say about where their journey was taking them.

We have been lacking for too long the quality of political leadership, a voice that will address the people directly, not just preach ideologies. The most alarming consequence was the emergence of what came to be known as a 'tête-à-tête society', the product of uncertainty and insecurity. It was not only that the old certainties reflected by the welfare system had begun to totter – the whole social consensus disintegrated. But the discussion of the causes and consequences took place in hushed tones. Rarely did anyone speak out. In the 1980s and 1990s there developed a clear division between the public debate, conducted in cryptic terms and dominated by half-truths and the unchallenged spread of illusions, and private discussions, where mistakes were freely acknowledged and sad truths openly confronted.

For example, politicians of the CDU and SPD share to a large extent a similar view of the development of the pensions system. The facts of the situation lead all experts to similar assessments. In private, they would be expected to consider fundamental changes in the system as inescapable. In public, however, they all continue to adhere to the principle of a state-run pensions system without any significant amendments.

The same is true of discussions about the reform of the universities. Experts of all parties and from all areas of education have long agreed that professors are facing radical cuts in their privileges and that the duration of courses urgently needs to be reduced. The students themselves have already faced up to the necessity of having to pay fees, provided that the money flows into the coffers of their own institution and is used to improve their conditions. In 'tête-à-tête' discussions the various political camps are probably closer to each other in their attitudes to controversial issues such as tax reform, welfare benefits and the crime figures relating to foreigners than public debates would imply, where distinctions are drawn not between what is sensible or foolish but between what is good and bad.

The development of this 'tête-à-tête' society has in the meantime become a huge problem for political parties themselves, not excluding the SPD. We must take heed of what Dieter Buhl wrote in *Die Zeit* on 1 October 1997: 'The situation demands frankness and honesty of all those who attach importance to the concept of the common good and who see the German Federal Republic neither as a nation dominated by corporations nor as an easy-going, soft-touch welfare state.'

This was also the sense in which many took the speech made by the former federal President Roman Herzog in Berlin on 26 April 1997, under the title 'Breaking into the Twenty-first Century'. In his address Herzog contrasted the social and economic dynamism that he had encountered on a trip to Asia with the air of despondency and the crisis scenarios he found in Germany. The knee-jerk reaction in favour of holding on to everything as it is, he said, made reform impossible. Jürgen Engert, television controller of the station Sender Freies Berlin, afterwards published a volume of reactions to Herzog's speech, cynically summarizing the conclusion of the occasion as follows: 'The final words had been spoken. The invited guests rose to their feet. Then one of them shouted at the top of his voice: "So much for the lecture! Now for the food!"' Public reaction in the days that followed took the same line. All agreed with Herzog's sentiments but no one thought his criticisms applied to them.

Ludwig Erhard commented in the 1960s that the superficial opinion that the Germans were good at creating prosperity but apparently incapable of controlling it was unfortunately more than a facile slogan. Today it is our duty to seek out every obstacle to progress and put every institution under the microscope. Impatient modernizers must range themselves against those who maintain there is no alternative to the status quo. Numerous well-thought-out projects have been put forward; there is plenty of scope for more flexible employment models within existing wage agreements. The public sector must be opened up to part-time work, combined with a comprehensive modernization of the state bureaucracy. It is perfectly feasible to work out special tariffs for the long-term unemployed and for subsidies for the low paid from the savings made in welfare funds. There is a need for investment in the infrastructure, as there is for a campaign to raise the numbers of qualified workers. The example set in the *Land* of North-Rhine-Westphalia should be extended over the country as a whole. In the last 40 years the proportion of self-employed workers has fallen from 17 to 7 per cent. The Germans have lost their entrepreneurial spirit. The introduction of an investment wage that would amount not just to a compulsory saving on the part of lower income groups would be one way of helping to restore this spirit.

These are only a few of the issues we could tackle straight-away. Also overdue is an agreed plan for more flexible and more intensive occupational training schemes, coupled with the closer integration of schools and industry, so that the promise originally given in North-Rhine-Westphalia, 'Every youngster who wants training will receive training', can be extended to the whole coun-try. Nor must the fight against youth unemployment be allowed to get bogged down in ideological arguments. When in 1997 the Young Socialists demanded that companies that did not offer places for trainees should be subject to a compulsory levy, the argument reached rock bottom – the advocacy of *dirigiste* policies that had been discredited time and again.

In every area of business, politics and social activity we con-tinue to cling to institutions and regulations, structures and pro-cedures which make it less and less possible for us to paint a clear picture of the social and economic changes that are taking place in an age of globalization, and to delineate and accommodate these changes. Rolf G. Heinze, a sociologist at the University of Bochum, described the situation in Germany as the crisis of a 'blocked society'. Our institutions and rules of procedure are losing their legitimacy because people are losing confidence in their ability to guarantee more security in times of increasing personal insecurity. Given their present structure, institutions such as polit-ical parties and trade unions are losing more and more support because potential members no longer believe that, with their traditional structures and routines, they are capable of keeping pace with the bewildering changes that they see going on around them every day. This applies equally to state systems like the retirement pension scheme and bodies that represent the inter-ests of business and of organized labour. There is a need to decentralize the exercise of power and responsibility and make it more flexible. At the same time there is also a need to establish a central consensus, combined with the guarantee of an increased degree of individual responsibility, according to the classical prin-ciple of subsidiarity. Moreover, this is a need felt by all the economic, social and political institutions in the country.

The endless arguments and discussions that went round and round in the 1980s resulted in many sensible and practicable schemes being sacrificed to the view that any plan for conceptual innovation represented an attack on the welfare state. Pragmatic proposals were simply regarded as irrelevant to any discussion concerned with the retention of the status quo. Fruitful debates on insurance for emergencies and old age, plans for a reform of the tax system and pension scheme – such proposals were put on the political agenda, thrashed out in one committee after another, then simply dropped. Even the subject of globalization, which should have given a spur to intelligent reforms, ended up by being ostentatiously ridiculed and demonized.

The first inklings of a looming crisis in employment and the social security system emerged in the 1980s and came, so to speak, from within. Nobody, no group in parliament, seriously challenged the rules that governed the philosophy of the welfare state. Indeed, a glance in the direction of the radical 'alternative', totalitarian socialism as practised behind the Iron Curtain, seemed all that was necessary to dispose of such a notion. All the parliamentary parties fell over each other in their eagerness to profess their loyalty to the concept of the status quo. This makes the break with the past so much more difficult. Globalization puts all the social and political institutions of individual nations to the rigid test of efficiency and functionality in the context of international competition, although it is by no means certain exactly what demands this globalization makes and how much room these demands leave for manoeuvre.

Globalization is a reality. It is experienced every day by German managers who have to confront foreign legal systems and deal with foreign markets. The world is shrinking. Individual nation-states seem to matter less and less. Polls show that almost three-quarters of German managers give it as their opinion that political events only appear to be in the forefront of world affairs – the real action is dominated by economic processes working behind the scenes. In all developed industrial nations the question of social cohesion, together with the ability to combine social security and economic efficiency, is arising in a new form. Globalization creates uncertainty where formerly everything appeared secure. To live in a country with many locational advantages and capable of competing in international markets is of itself no longer a guarantee of a safe job. Indeed, the employment situation in such countries seems to be more insecure than ever. In industries like steel, where competition is only over price,

German workers suddenly find themselves facing direct competition from workers on the other side of the world, whom, unlike their foreign colleagues in their own factories, they will never get to see or assess. Germany's national frontiers no longer offer any protection against the consequences of international competition.

Under headings such as the international division of labour and the transnationalization or internationalization of companies, we have been discussing the transfer of resources, production, capital and, to a lesser extent, labour from one economy to another for as long as we have been able to identify what we call 'the world economy'. Such discussions have gone hand in hand with industrialization. But the theory of the international division of labour is no longer adequate to explain the regional policies of international corporations. The changes that have taken place over the last fifteen to twenty years have been too great – the increasing irrelevance of national barriers as a result of the explosion of telecommunications, the integration of data-processing, information technology and material communicated via the global internet. Information technology itself has become a central factor in production, in which time and distance are no object to the conduct of trade, sending formerly 'place-bound' services all over the world, twenty-four hours a day, heedless of time zones.

Politics must adjust itself to management strategies which organize worldwide combines. In place of national labels such as 'Made in Germany' we shall have 'Made by Daimler' or 'Made by Lufthansa'. We are facing radically different global patterns of international trade which are, in the last analysis, no longer natural or sectoral divisions of labour between economies. When new products, services or processes take the place of the old, we must see to it that we are in the forefront of development. Once left behind, there is no chance to catch up.

In the automobile industry the Japanese had to undertake numerous innovative developments before being in a position to launch a car that would be successful in the European market. In microtechnology, and especially in the software industry, this is no longer true, as was shown a few years ago by the example of Bangalore, in India, which rapidly became the software capital of the world. Jobs created by a German firm in Portugal can help to preserve and create jobs in Germany, provided we make the most of each locality and integrate production, thereby becoming competitive in international markets.

In the meantime, global cross-border investment has been growing three times faster than trade. Between 1984 and 1990 alone exports of capital by the most important industrialized nations have increased fourfold. New export records contrast with stagnating investment at home, rapidly growing German direct investment abroad with sluggish and reluctant investment in Germany itself. Meanwhile international capital markets have entered a new age. In 1980 the value of cross-border trade in bonds and securities amounted to less than a tenth of the gross domestic product of the leading industrialized countries; in 1997, stimulated by dealings in 'real time', it far outstripped the performance of all these countries put together. On the world currency markets alone the daily turnover in the main trading currencies of some $US1.2 billion has reached about 20 per cent of annual exports worldwide. Less than 5 per cent of currency dealings are based on actual economic transactions – the remainder consists merely of financial transactions in which risks and returns are the yardstick.

The exponential growth in international commercial, manufacturing and financial dealings is strikingly demonstrated by the statement from the UN Conference on Trade and Development (UNCTAD) that in 1997 there was a worldwide economic network embracing 39,000 multinational concerns, plus some 270,000 subsidiary companies. The world export quota rose from about 7 per cent of gross domestic product worldwide in 1950 to 15 per cent in 1973 and to 22.5 per cent today. Irrespective of the extent to which the visions of international corporations may or may not have been realized, the megatrend of globalization is a fact and dominates the scene.

In the public debate the complex phenomenon of globalization has been reduced to a competition over costs. For all the complexity of the phenomenon itself, the logic behind the debate is straightforward. Companies produce in areas where costs are lowest – taxes, welfare contributions and wages. At the same time there is a shift in the strategy of international firms from the search for new markets to methods of reducing costs. This is accompanied by a move on the part of industrial concerns to seek additional profits in expanding capital markets, profits now less easily made in their traditional areas. In this respect business and management practices have left macroeconomic theories well behind as far as their assessment of globalization processes is concerned.

Governments, on the other hand, which are not involved in the competition between national and regional localities for companies and supply companies, and consequently can offer favourable wage costs, a transparent tax system with low rates of tax, and reduced welfare contributions, appear to be in danger of finding their fields of activity reduced to arid territories offering no jobs, no tax revenue and no future.

To conclude, however, that globalization spells the end for the state and for politics, leaving no scope for manoeuvre, would be premature. For the most destructive aspect of the globalization debate is that it destroys our shared political arena. It makes people believe that there is no area of life left in which, through the agency of their elected representatives, they can devise effective and acceptable rules for coexistence, in particular for the economy. Put in exaggerated terms: legislation is passed in Brussels, while the decision about my job is taken in the head office of some corporation on the other side of the world, in response to pressure from anonymous capital markets and analysts. What is the point of voting, being creative and constructive, demonstrating solidarity? And what is the use of the right to vote, to join a political party, or an association, or a Church? The globalization debate has destroyed the tangible reality of politics and any confidence we had of being able to influence events.

This applied in particular to the preparations for European economic and currency union. The Social Democrats have shouldered the task of helping to make the union a success and at the same time to bring Europe closer to its citizens. It is a paradoxical situation. Those who warned of the dangers of introducing the euro too hastily, and never shared the enthusiastic view that it would automatically create jobs, are now bent on making it a success, an honest currency. The debate on the euro conducted by politicians and in the media, which more than any other issue needed to be conducted soberly and objectively, had already by 1997 taken on the character of a pitched battle, a religious war in which one could only choose 'between cholera and the plague', between a soft currency and economic particularism. The neurotic discussions about the date for the start of the single currency and the criteria for taking part in the project were a bad omen. Judged by the events of 1996 and 1997, the debate on Europe and the euro offered no strategic answers to the challenges of the new age but was characterized by nationalistic timidity.

People of my generation, and those of the younger generation even more so, regard Europe as a natural part of their lives, not the price of their history or a decision between war and peace, but an opportunity for the future. The link between economic policy and European policy is becoming closer and closer, while discussions and decisions taken with the European Commission – on matters such as the effects of the reform of the structure of the EU on individual *Länder* such as North-Rhine-Westphalia – have long been matters of course for the economics ministers of the *Länder*, and far more important than negotiations with the federal government. Economic conditions in the regions and the *Länder* are basically determined in Brussels. Our policies must emphasize the enormous economic and social opportunities that the European Union offers, but also the conditions that will have to be met if these opportunities are to be grasped. A common European currency can strengthen the hand of the European Union in global competition with other economic regions of the world, give us more influence over world economic policies and make a contribution to a comprehensive world financial and trade system. For Germany itself new opportunities will be created when the pressure of exchange rates on export-oriented businesses disappears.

By virtue of its responsibility for overseas trade, the EU was able to assert its influence in Uruguay and resist the amalgamation of Boeing and McDonald-Douglas, and will also be a powerful voice in negotiations over currency parities. The tragedy of the German national economy is that it does not recognize the role that power – both today and in the future – still plays in the economy.

There is without doubt a global need for a second world currency. Seen in this light, the single European currency offers the last chance for the Old World to assert itself. It will also create financial markets that are less prone to crises. The Netherlands are backing the euro, among other reasons, because with a wider financial market and more favourable interest rates the scope for refinancing of public corporations will be greater than it is on the present limited national financial markets.

True, in 1997 Gerhard Schröder drew attention to the risks attached to the euro and was widely criticized for dubbing the common currency 'a premature baby' which needed careful nurturing. But one thing is certain – the euro will not solve our employment problems. There are sectors in which existing jobs are coming under pressure more quickly than new jobs can be created in other sectors. The adjustments which the German economy, especially small and medium-sized firms and the EU administration, is looking for will not come about of their own accord but must be made one of the main subjects of our future policies. The fight against tax dumping needs to be put on the agenda, so does the harmonization of all systems, from the welfare system to the environment. Not for nothing did the International Monetary Fund draw attention in 1998 to the risks facing the euro in German domestic politics. In particular, the lack of a German employment policy could, in the eyes of many foreign observers, have destabilizing effects in the long term. The persistently high rate of unemployment in Germany can prove as severe a threat to the stability of the single currency as the financial problems facing other countries.

The root of these problems lies not in the levels of debt of individual countries but in the sluggish pace of the creation of economic and fiscal union, with its supranational monetary policy and a corresponding inadequate harmonization of economic, financial and employment policies. In October 1991 Chancellor Helmut Kohl stated in the Bundestag: 'It cannot be repeated too often: political union is the inevitable counterpart of economic and currency union. Recent history has taught us that the idea that there could be a lasting economic and currency union without political union is mistaken.' At that time there was a fashionable phrase going the rounds that talked of the euro as 'setting the crown' on economic union – both a culmination and a conclusion. But this never came about. Our task now is not to shed tears over what might have been but to make up for lost time.

If we are to grasp the opportunities that a European single currency undoubtedly offers, we need not only a sufficient convergence of the various national economies but a harmonization of national economic policies. The stability aimed at by the European central bank requires supporting measures in fiscal, taxation and employment policy. A thoroughgoing reform of the institutional decision-making mechanisms and an overhaul of the efficiency of the European Commission itself are essential – and not only within the framework of Maastricht III, IV or V. The Maastricht Treaty did not lay down how each individual country was to achieve the stability of its currency – each country had to work it out for itself. The same applies to the Social Democrats' demands for measures to counter welfare dumping. The majority of our European neighbours cannot match our high standards, and the Union includes countries with markedly differing levels of welfare benefits.

Therefore we need different 'channels' of social security within which countries can refer to each other and aim at a convergence of their standards – so-called harmonization. With unemployment at 3.2 per cent in Luxemburg and 22.2 per cent in Spain, there is no way in which Europe can count on producing a unified social and employment policy, but neither can it afford to leave an individual country to solve its problems by itself.

We also need a harmonization of taxation, particularly in the case of cross-border corporate taxation, for we must prevent businesses from being encouraged to transfer the headquarters of their operations from one country to another on the grounds of favourable dumping offers. The Maastricht code of conduct does not go far enough as long as it fails to make clear what national practices are considered to constitute 'harmful' rivalry in taxation matters, and as long as exceptional budgetary surpluses threaten to flood the scene. The essence of the situation is that without measures to combat mass unemployment in Europe there will not in the long run be a stable euro. If we want to grasp the opportunities created by a single currency, there is only one way – namely, to join a free, democratic, federal union, open in foreign policy, liberal in domestic policy, which combines cultural, linguistic and ethnic variety with basic elements of European political unity. Integration will only take place in cases where individual states are not able to handle the situation by themselves and where co-operation on an administrative level is not sufficient. European economic and currency union offers the opportunity for states to learn from each other through pragmatic solutions. It is the biggest benchmarking exercise in history.

Globalization and the European Union spell the end for all ideological schools of thought. From flexible and part-time working arrangements to a proactive social and employment policy and the creation of intelligent supply-side policies 'from the left', we are in desperate need of new, intelligent answers which are, when necessary, prepared to ride roughshod over the formulae found in the party programmes. My own attitude towards globalization and the progressive integration of the national states of Europe is this: between indisputable economic trends and the people there have always been filters which render the effects of modernization bearable and convert these effects into agencies of social progress. The history of the welfare state is a case in point. But the state and corporate institutions from which we expect this are in part as old as the model itself. Their capacity for adaptation is considerable but was left to stagnate for too long, causing structures to atrophy and so-called 'established proced-ures' to act as a brake on progress. Solidarity and social security are also among the imperatives of the global market but in new forms.

Our task is to rebuild and breathe new life into traditional institutions, not to undermine them. In the summer of 1997, in the wake of an escalating debate as dramatic as it was inevitable, Germany itself experienced an attack on the constitution of the Federal Republic. The gauntlet was thrown down to federalism, which was held to be responsible for political and social stagna-tion, a taunt provoked by the age-old accusation levelled by every government at the opposition when it has a majority in the Bundesrat, the second chamber – the taunt of 'blocking tactics'. In view of the stagnation and the blockade that the government itself had caused, this shifting of the blame on to the Bundesrat was a tactical manoeuvre. Hans-Olaf Henkel, chairman of the German Confederation of Industries, who showed himself willing to carry the attack against the *Länder* into the public arena, was acting in the interests of those firms that were engaged in global competition, and certainly not out of hostility to the constitu-tion. His attack was at best naive. But it missed its target. For a debate under the slogan 'Employers Against Federalism' only repeats a discussion that took place in the late 1920s in Germany, and in view of unmistakeable trends towards Europeanization – *pace* corresponding tendencies to regionalization – is hardly relevant to the present day. Indeed, the reforming nations of Europe have recognized the essential political, social and economic weakness of the centralized state. Not only for reasons of integra-tion do we see attempts to introduce a higher degree of decen-tralization, more regional autonomy and other modifications to the federal system.

The debate that took place in the 1920s showed how little was achieved by initiatives undertaken by private coteries of employers. The steel magnate Paul Reusch, together with Hans

Luther, Reich Chancellor in 1925–6 and President of the Reichs-
bank from 1930 to 1933, and others set out to reform the
country by restricting federalism, limiting the scope of wage agreements and generally reducing the power of the parliamentary
system. Faced with a crisis in the economy, they saw a crisis
in the democratic structures of the country as a whole and de-
nounced the state for its inability to make decisions among the
confusion of conflicting interests that surrounded it – a situation
that is not unlike today. To some, it also appears as though in
times of crisis the federal, liberal, parliamentary constitutional
state itself produces a state of ungovernability – albeit with one
difference, namely that at that time none of those involved were
friends of the constitution. Reusch and his companions would
have been delighted to dispense with the whole parliamentary
system, including the Reichstag itself.

Today, things are different. Nobody seriously thinks of abolishing the Bundesrat. But in the 1920s the legitimacy of the young
federal Weimar Republic was so profoundly undermined that
its opponents had no difficulty in bringing about its demise. And
we all know what followed.

At the same time Henkel was not so far from the truth. Like
all institutions, federalism has to ask itself what it wishes to
achieve and what it ought to achieve. In West Germany an extensive 'compensatory federalism' has developed, distinguished
by a levelling-out of all incentives. A marked tendency on the
part of the federal government to extend its area of competence
is balanced by a growing compensatory trend to allow the provincial governments a larger degree of participation in central
discussions on conceptual matters and in basic decisions on broad
European issues. The *Länder* governments themselves were left
with continually diminishing areas of competence, with the result that the confidence of these governments in their ability to
deal with matters that fell within their own jurisdiction also
declined, which, in turn, together with the redistribution of income between central government, provincial governments and
local authorities, stifled their initiative and ultimately their feeling
of being directly responsible for the control of their own affairs.
This compensatory policy, in its present form, is partly responsible for the fact that we have hitherto been unable to develop a
viable form of that 'competitive federalism' that we urgently need.

In many fields the multiplicity of joint committees of representatives from the federal and the provincial governments has

produced a kind of 'hypercoordination'. The most important question is, can we live with a form of federalism that (a) does not make 'equality of opportunity' a cardinal principle; (b) for which economic egalitarianism is not the beginning and the end of the affair; and (c) whose principles and raison-d'être lie in pursuing the best solutions within a competitive system? In the regional policies of North-Rhine-Westphalia we have experienced, since the beginning of the 1980s, an increasing importance of the regions in economic dealings within a competitive Europe. Economic and social cohesion in Europe forces us to make clear concessions in respect of our exaggerated expectations of uniformity. And vice versa: for the regions, much will depend on how the principle of subsidiarity is revised and what political aims the EU is planning to pursue in this regard.

This makes it all the more essential to abandon the 'negative co-ordination' of the federal system as soon as possible and evolve a viable distribution of powers which will produce more incentives in the competition between the various *Länder*. Any form of centralized control in Europe is doomed to failure. In its place we need a creative federalism that will clearly identify goals, financial implications and individual areas of responsibility. I can even conceive of a European army.

Cultural policy, on the other hand, can and must be in essence a regional concern, albeit with a degree of co-ordination exercised by the new federal Director of Culture. Education policy, in turn, should to a large extent be Europeanized, so that qualifications can be harmonized. But nothing would be more superfluous than a federal Ministry of Education. Education must be focused on the regions and the EU, with an emphasis on international mobility.

Federalism itself is what one makes it. Given a new context, it could become more modern than ever. The USA, Spain and the UK are all trying to revive the concept of federalism, which might well offer hope of a solution to the problem of Northern Ireland as well. The German Bundesrat must make it its task to stimulate and co-ordinate the efforts of the *Länder* to organize their own affairs and solve their own problems.

This becomes particularly clear in the field of economic policy. In international competition the economic importance of so-called 'hard' local factors is declining because we can now take them everywhere for granted. More important is the development of an individual local profile, made up of the quality of the schools,

universities, training colleges, etc., practical research and technological advances, co-operation between small, medium and large
businesses, the intelligent planning of passenger and freight transportation systems and, finally, the whole communications infrastructure, not forgetting cultural factors. How easy it is to support
the establishment of small and medium-sized businesses, how
easy it is to raise venture capital, how flexible and innovative
planning authorities are, how efficiently communications systems
are linked up with each other – all this is decided in the individual *Land*. Every third job in a particular region springs not
from central planning but from local factors. It is one of the
striking consequences of globalization that the whole world may
come to know of a small area – perhaps only a valley, like Silicon
Valley – that has become the centre of attraction for the world's
leading manufacturers of particular products. Specialization and
top quality have often made the fortune of a small region as a
result of globalization. Inferior quality loses out. The regions
must constantly be urged to rise to the challenge of innovation,
in both conceptual and practical respects.

In this context, as far as Germany is concerned, it is North-
Rhine-Westphalia that has set the pace. Other examples can be
found in the area of foreign trade, where individual *Länder* have
been involved in creating jobs in Singapore and elsewhere. Today
there are more important things to do than reorganize the *Länder*,
especially as there would be no political majority on which to
call, and certainly no majority in favour of such a move among
the people at large.

All the processes and institutions that are being blamed today
for the blockages in society and in political life can be reversed
or reprogrammed. We have taken up cudgels against those who
claim there is no alternative way. We must revitalize politics, and
the SPD, in particular, must open its door to all those who judge
things by results, subscribe to the motto 'A small deed is better
than big words', and derive their moral standards for political
action from concrete events. To say, in times when we are facing
immense problems, 'it was well meant', is fatal. The only thing
that counts in practical politics is what is 'well done.'

I am an implacable opponent of the defence of the status quo
because, as the pressure builds, even the most modest innovation for dealing with the problems has to be forced through, even
when the solution does not square with one's own principles.

Politicians who defend the status quo of the welfare state to the bitter end are in fact consigning the welfare state to the grave. They are facing the wrong way, like those laissez-faire critics who are out not to reform the welfare state but to dismantle it. The composer Richard Wagner once said, 'To be German is to do something for its own sake.' This German weakness must not be allowed to hinder the search for pragmatic solutions to practical problems. To see in the prospect of change only risks and not opportunities is to prevent people from taking the prompt action that is necessary.

The disintegration of a working society and the disaster of the funding of the social security system constitute together the most predictable crisis of the century, anticipated in numerous studies published in the 1980s. As far as the retirement pension system is concerned, the demographic pattern has been known for over twenty years. The effects of globalization on businesses and on the economy were described years ago, while the debate on 'the end of productive work' and the crisis surrounding the industrial society dates from the beginning of the 1980s. In other words, there was no shortage of proposals for dealing with the situation. Similarly, there have been many suggestions on how to tackle the problems that have arisen over the last ten years – the introduction of flexible working on a large scale, the extension of opportunities for low-skill workers and the unemployed through new initial wage rates and wage subsidies, etc.

But when we look around, we find that other countries have long put into practice what in Germany we have been discussing for the past fifteen years. While the Netherlands, for instance, were putting reforms in place, the Germans were sitting round the table – and still are. What is needed is a rigorous policy of pragmatism to get to the root of our problems. Count Otto Lambsdorff, one-time Economics Minister, said in his final address as economics spokesman for the Free Democrats that every economic and finance policy must be judged by the effect it is seen to have on the labour market – and he was right.

There are three 'blockages' that need to be cleared out of the system. First: the often-cited 'Rhenish' co-operation model is in a serious state of crisis – not because a fudged consensus cut short any further attempt to find a solution, but because today co-operation is limited to an ability to make only minimal compromises between one's own position and that of one's opponents.

The result is co-operation as a calculated tactic, concerned not with reaching common goals but with abstruse questions of power. The position of the side that makes the first move to regain its constructive freedom is weakened. In such rituals all institutions are accused of thinking only of their own interests, even the traditional institutions involved in negotiations and mediation. The failure of the first labour alliance, created in 1996, which met with the resistance of the former coalition government under Helmut Kohl, showed that the ability of the employers, the unions, the parties and parliament to exercise their responsibility for the welfare of the public is under threat. The same can be seen in the crisis facing professional associations and the churches. Today, a single-issue public campaign is an easier method of getting one's way than pursuing the issue through the established channels.

Secondly, one must dispose of the mistaken conception that the state is an obstacle to dynamic development in the economy and in society within a context of globalization. The shibboleth is deregulation. Because they did not have the strength to base their policies on new values and new conceptions and force these policies through against the resistance of entrenched interests, the conservatives adopted the policy time and again after 1982 of pleading *force majeure*, quoting circumstances sometimes imagined, sometimes invented.

The third institutional obstacle became evident when, in 1996, after the collapse of the Alliance for Employment, a negative campaign was launched, based on the principle of putting as many impediments in the path of one's opponents as possible. As in the popular board game called 'Malice', it is less important to be first past the post than to block the progress of the other players. When the game, a subtle variant of Ludo, was launched in 1960, it aroused a great deal of interest. Today, as popular as ever, it has another relevance. At the beginning of 1996, trade unions, chambers of commerce, politicians and officials from North-Rhine-Westphalia got round the table to work out a voluntary deal through which to tackle the long overdue reform of the dual system and provide an apprenticeship for everybody who wanted one. This caused a howl of protest from the leaders of organizations in Bonn. 'Out of the question!' they cried. 'Suppose every school-leaver applied!' It was the 'Malice' factor at work, blocking any attempt to formulate new strategies and initiatives. It led to a fear of taking risks, intolerant attitudes to anyone who made a mistake and an inability to learn on the part of companies, parties and bureaucracies. It is a syndrome familiar to those who have researched the psychology of innovation.

There is a parallel to this to be found in a zoological experiment. If one puts a frog into hot water, it will immediately jump out. If, however, one puts it into cold water and gradually brings the water to boiling-point, the frog will remain sitting there until it is cooked.

Time is running out. The social market economy has not failed. But there is a call for us to return to its principles. The loss of confidence in our economic system must be stopped. At the end of August 1997 two sociologists from Mannheim, Matthias Jung and Dieter Roth, conducted a representative poll on behalf of the Association of German Banks and came to an alarming conclusion about the state of political confidence in Germany. From what the 2,000 interviewees stated, it became clear that all scenarios aimed at blocking reform – from the weakness of elites and the failure of the political parties to the general grumbling of a disaffected society and the painful modernization of the corporate sector – had produced a loss of confidence such as Germany had never known. Faced with economic problems and political stagnation, 60 per cent of the population believe that the country is ill-prepared to meet the challenges of the future – which says less about the competitiveness of the German economy than about the relationship between the country's citizens and their political leaders.

The Germans have long learned to put two and two together. Three-quarters are of the opinion that the last federal government lacked the energy and determination to rise above the conflicting interests of individual factions and lobbies. Out of twelve public bodies, starting with the police and the federal constitutional court, the government and the political parties occupy eleventh and twelfth places in the public's perception of their ability to solve the country's problems. The message is clear: people are failing to identify a political force that will tell them in which direction the country is going. Political leadership could, however, not only produce solutions to practical problems but also regain the confidence of the population, for over 80 per cent consider strong leadership to be a condition for the survival of democracy in Germany. In August 1998 the journal *Capital* published the results of a poll taken among leading intellectuals in the Allensbach Institute for Demoscopy. The poll showed that 46 per cent regarded the government and the opposition as equally responsible for the political inertia. Criticism was also levelled at the trade unions and the workers. Two-thirds described the relationship between unions and management as 'poor' rather than 'satisfactory', and believed that it had got worse over recent years – to the detriment of the unemployed.

Polls clearly indicate that the crisis scenarios put out day after day in the media have served to consolidate a pessimistic outlook on the way the world is going, even in areas where a degree of enterprise and personal initiative is still to be found. Although 70 per cent of the German population tend to be optimistic about their own prospects for the future, when asked about the mood of the majority of other Germans, two-thirds preferred to call it 'not optimistic'. While 90 per cent were satisfied with their lives, over half were afraid that there would be growing discontent in society as a whole. And 80 per cent were of the opinion that the Germans complain too much. An overwhelming majority considered that the days when they enjoyed the highest wages, the shortest working week and the longest vacations were over and done with. 'As things stand,' they say, 'things are all right. But if we continue this way, we shall go downhill.'

Given the conflicting perceptions at home and abroad and the nation's fixation on the issue of security, the question arises: what demands are people prepared to put up with? Both in the east and the west there is general agreement that the state cannot raise the money it needs to plug the holes in the budget by raising taxes. Nor is an increase in state borrowing advocated. Instead, people propose the sale of bonds and reductions in government spending. The former does not hurt the individual, while the latter leaves the hope that one will be spared such cuts oneself. When the question is raised of where the cuts are to be made, people list welfare benefits, unemployment benefit and benefits for asylum seekers. It is not an accident that these are areas in which the majority of those polled would in any case not be affected by such cuts.

What is one to make of such selfish demands and paradoxical attitudes? It is tempting to see them as clear proof of the mental block that afflicts a society whose mind-sets can only be cleared of their cobwebs by a blast of cold air from the real world of competition. At the same time it is vital that a willingness to accept change is closely linked to the ability of the political class to take the lead. The results of the study undertaken by Jung and Roth bring us down to earth. But they also make clear that conditions are favourable for reform if only politicians and political parties will get rid of the psychological blockages in their own ranks. Germany has for too long conducted it politics in an atmosphere of anxiety. We must take those seriously who fear that the carefully calculated and delicate balance between freedom and community spirit will be lost – the view expressed in the slogan 'Economization of politics and society'. But it cannot be meant in that sense – rather, in the sense that in future no solution, no instrument of state intervention, can be allowed to be uneconomic. Survival into the next century will depend on the principle of economicality, applied to the aim of financing a humane society. The marketplace is not an end in itself but a means to an end. At the same time the whole range of social policies can profit from a study of economic logic if they are geared to produce specific results in the employment field and are measured against this aim.

Citizens have an unfulfilled, albeit unpredictable, need to identify with their state. Since the beginning of the 1980s people have been unable to reconcile politics and government actions with the terms of their day-to-day life. It is their declining confidence in the ability of politicians to solve the problems confronting us, not doubts about the model itself, that characterizes the identity crisis of the social market economy. The Allensbach findings confirm both: on the one hand, the loss of confidence in the economic order to which West Germany owes its economic recovery after the Second World War, and on the other, rising hopes of higher achievements. The ideals of Ludwig Erhard are in vogue, whereas there is a declining confidence that the state will be capable of opening up new fields in which these ideals can flourish.

Until about ten years ago the Germans were convinced that the market economy and the welfare system had existed peacefully side by side in a complementary relationship. It was this balance that people credited with maintaining the credibility of the system – efficiency balanced by humanity. The achievement of success and the acceptance of competition – these were their aims. Over 70 per cent subscribed to the principle 'Competition is a good thing – it makes people work hard and develop new ideas.'

A clear majority was similarly in favour of offering greater incentives to higher productivity (at the expense of a reduction of wage differentials). It was assumed that prosperity would grow 'until there was enough for everyone', while each individual would have to shoulder more self-responsibility. In a poll conducted by the Emnid organization in January 1997, 56 per cent of those questioned between 14 and 29 years of age replied that they would prefer to be self-employed. But almost half also believed that hard work did not guarantee success – it was more a matter of luck or of having the right contacts. People had to make the painful discovery that performance no longer led to success in every case, and that conscientiousness and sacrifice did not add to one's personal sense of security or enable one to plan one's career with greater confidence. Seen from this angle, the social component of the social market economy is far from amounting to the full provisions of the complete welfare state. That social component now takes a different form: individual achievement is rewarded and guaranteed by growing prosperity; the acquisition of further qualifications is rewarded by promotion; a willingness to assume greater responsibility is rewarded by a wider scope for economic activities; and self-employment is rewarded by a guaranteed second chance if things were to fail.

According to the Allensbach survey, half the population today think Erhard 'planned constructively for the future' and displayed great vision. Asked, however, in November 1996 whether any of toady's politicians would be capable of creating a new 'economic miracle', only 8.2 per cent said 'Yes'.

It was a revealing moment, one deserving of further investigation, when in the anniversary year of 1997 parties and other institutions vied with each other in claiming to be the true heirs of Ludwig Erhard, architect of the German 'Economic Miracle'. The most outspoken wrangling took place between welfare ministers and free enterprise economists. Norbert Blüm, CDU Minister for Employment, trumpeted that it was not Adam Smith who had proved Marx wrong, but Ludwig Erhard. Otto Lambsdorff retorted that an overladen welfare state was exactly what Erhard had not wanted. That Erhard's skill lay precisely in striking a balance between economic and welfare policies, and maintaining it, was entirely overlooked. If he were alive today, he would read the riot act to many of those who celebrated him, men responsible for mass unemployment, weak investment, the high incidence of bankruptcies, taxes at record levels and so on. When people today talk of the 'Economic Miracle', they are more likely to be thinking of the United States of America and its 'Employment Miracle' than of Germany in the years following the end of the Second World War.

I am realistic about this. Ludwig Erhard did not leave the Social Democrats anything in his will. But his heirs have frittered away his heritage and his ideas have been abandoned. His name may fairly be invoked in connection with the contemporary policies of the Social democrats, and his ideas exploited. He will stand as one of the pillars that carry the bridge which links liberal principles to the basic values of the SPD, thereby forming a powerful and rational synthesis of interests. At the centre of this synthesis lies the reconstruction of the social market economy, of which Erhard's timeless principles are the cornerstones. His reply to 'Workers of the world, unite!' was 'Prosperity for all!' And his demand won the day.

But all this is history. Today we are facing the consequences of globalization, and the vital question is: are we capable not only of offering an alternative to a different conception of the state but also, over and above this, of resisting the threat of the dwindling competence of the state to control affairs and bringing forward new concepts of our own? Today, Erhard's cry would be 'A job for everybody!'

Erhard represents much that is important as a new millennium dawns. There is, for example, his principle of the state as a self-confident, proactive force which allows market forces free rein but at the same time retains a careful balance between them. A withdrawal from all active intervention, as practised by the German coalition government between 1981 and 1998, would have been unthinkable under Erhard. An opponent of all ideologies but a man of firm principles, he was at heart a liberal who saw the state as the creator and guardian of an ordered framework within which market forces could freely interact but also in which the impact on society as a whole must not be lost sight of for a single minute. It is not a question of less government or more government, but of a strong state with the power to compel rival partners to come together in cases of conflict of interest which threaten to get out of control. This too is a principle more relevant today than ever.

During the time, 1945–6, when he was Economics Minister in the provincial government of Bavaria, Erhard saw that state direction and collective planning were not the answer. His urgent concern was to find a conciliatory formula which would combine the findings of economics with the contemporary demands of society. The term adopted was 'social market economy', coined by Alfred Müller-Armack, a minister in Erhard's ministry. Since that time the debate has continued to simmer over what place the social element in the market economy should occupy. One thing, however, is clear. A successful economics policy – assuming a broad distribution of property – should keep the need for social intervention to a minimum. At the same time, the minimalization of state intervention in social matters is no substitute for an efficient economic policy. The blunt fact is, we have to earn what we can spend.

On the other hand, social policy is more than a guarantor of people's losses. It must put people in a position where they can co-operate in the plan. Its aim is to reconcile economic efficiency with the needs of the labour market. The emphasis on employment that Gerhard Schröder made part of his programme, and his view of the scope of the actions that government can take to deal with it, would have met with Erhard's approval. Schröder asked the question, namely: what is the point of an economics policy if it is not to give people jobs and enable them to earn a living?

The second basic principle of economic policy should be to dispense with all kinds of ideology in favour of a rigorous pragmatism. In his biography of Erhard, Volker Hentschel made the ironical remark that Erhard was perhaps so gifted a politician because he was so bad an economist. This is an almost complimentary dig at the pragmatic policies adopted by Erhard, who at the beginning of the 1970s defined the social market economy as 'a means of combining a firm exterior framework with a wealth of individual creative possibilities within it'. The social market economy is like a voyage of discovery in the course of which new opportunities and procedures are continually being tried out. As far as economic policy is concerned, this means not clinging to old, rigid tenets but calling on principles and possibilities which have already proven their empirical value in many areas. Erhard vigorously opposed the facile assumption that with the help of a handful of government measures we could buck the trend of history.

Erhard's view is more relevant today than ever. Whether, on the right, we hear stereotyped sermons preaching that globalization is compelling us to restrict the scope for political action, or, on the left, there are voices calling for a return to the old doctrines of redistributive economics and *dirigiste* politics – in both cases the end result is a return to ideological solutions, which only leave the confused citizen facing a solution that is no solution. The left seems to have the answers when the question of redistribution is raised, because it has a policy of participation; when it is a matter of economic growth, on the other hand, the conservatives seem to hold the cards, because they know more about business. All this is old hat. Concentrating on solving problems, ignoring any resolutions that may have been passed in party meetings and challenging everything that blocks progress in the development of our society – such is the only moral way forward. The nature of our policies will be decided by the substance of those policies. Today's Social Democratic Party stands for ethical action, an ethic of dynamic advance. That is the commitment on the part of a German and European left-wing party that has abjured ideology.

Whether the SPD will be able to develop the anti-*dirigiste* principles of the social market economy to modernize the state on all levels is a question of confidence. In the course of the modernization process, both of the party itself and of the state, the party will have to evolve a completely new kind of political approach. The nanny state has had its day; what we now need is a proactive state which promotes the values of modernization and introduces innovations into social life. We must take our lead from people's resources and skills, not be held back by their deficiencies. Wherever there is social and economic dynamism, there the state must be active. The economic and social challenges facing us can only be solved co-operatively and by consensus, through concerted action both at federal and regional level. The most important moments of modernization will come with the formation of 'innovation task forces', when employers, trade unions, politicians, civil servants and other groups in society will meet round the table to discuss how modernization can be made a reality.

There is no better figure to symbolize the spirit of confidence and revival in times of stress and difficulty than Ludwig Erhard. The search for solutions can be based on his principles. 'Instead of stumbling about in a social and political no man's land,' he wrote, 'we should make it our aim, tomorrow even more than today, to think clearly and soberly about the problems that confront us.' It is a demand more urgent today than ever.

This invocation of the figure of Ludwig Erhard does not provide an excuse to return to old, familiar ways but is intended as a means of drawing attention to the possibility of innovation and modernization. During the years of the CDU–FDP coalition government, principles were abandoned that were holy to Erhard – consensus and co-operation, calculated intervention in place of laissez-faire, pragmatism in economic policy. All those who identify with the ethos of the social market economy are looking for a return to these values – tradesmen, the middle classes, the self-employed and owners of small businesses. At a time when there is a lack of moral and political leadership, people are longing for comprehensive and credible programmes and for leaders who are not bound by formalism, ideology and the cultivation of sectional interests. This collective recourse to the value of the 'Economic Miracle', which we regularly experience at moments of crisis, represents simply our desire for a viable model.

2

The Maxims of
a Proactive State

During the period of the Cold War the West European welfare state was never seriously put to the test, not even – at least to start with – when it got into financial difficulties and when a growing individualization and pluralization in private life and in working conditions tested the validity of the structure of the various welfare systems. The West German system, both in its democratic ethos and its economic superiority, was so manifestly preferable to what was found in the socialist East that it seemed unnecessary to consider any alternative. But the end of the East–West conflict has meant that the convenient way of defining one's own political and social identity by a positive comparison with the negative features of the East German model is no longer possible.

As the conflict between East and West, a force which had made for stability on the political scene, came to an end, the crisis in the world of the Western democracies, in the traditional parties of left and right alike, became apparent. By the middle of the 1970s the strategies of the social democratic welfare state had outlived their usefulness. For after the Second World War a policy had evolved, even where the Social Democrats were not in control, which in effect aimed at distributing the profits of economic growth according to political and social criteria, restricting competition and attaching great importance to state intervention. For this one historic moment no other kind of policies seemed conceivable in the Western democracies.

When this more or less homogeneous model of the welfare state found itself confronting a crisis, and the Germans awoke from their 'brief dream of permanent prosperity', as Ralf Dahrendorf called it, there came 'the end of the social democratic century'. The electors deserted the parties in droves, charging them with being responsible for high insurance deductions and with being authoritarian. When the CDU–FDP coalition came into power in 1982, it embarked on a policy of cut-backs and restoring the influence of competition and market forces.

Then, towards the middle of the 1990s, conservative governments in their turn found themselves in difficulties, unable to keep mounting debts under control, while social inequality increased yet economic growth remained sluggish. Such was the situation in Germany as well. But the change of direction announced by the new CDU-led government, which it claimed was characterized by widespread deregulation, in fact ended up as an unstoppable drive for new regulations and a plethora of new laws. Further so-called reforms amounted in large measure merely to reductions in welfare benefits, which, however, made little impression on the structural crisis facing the welfare state, because they did not reflect any new basic policy. Time and again such actions had to be put down to 'internal pressures' – the costs of reunification, measures needed to ensure conformity with the provisions of the Maastricht Treaty, etc. – in order to bring about a gradual dismantling of the welfare state against the interests of its citizens. For this reason German politics seems today to consist of nothing more than a one-sided distribution of financial burdens.

Since the end of the 1970s we have lost sight of the concrete question: what are the political means by which Germany can effect, promote and guarantee economic and social change – and, above all, a coherent philosophical infrastructure to underpin the adoption of such means? In the 1980s and the first half of the 1990s people found themselves faced with an alternative that was no alternative. On the one hand, more planning and controls, ever more expensive programmes to cure the symptoms of the disease, ever more money for the state: then, they were told, all would be well. On the other hand, deregulation at all costs, the dismantling of the welfare state and the transfer of all political decision-making to international bodies. Since the middle of the 1990s the battle-line has been drawn up between the embattled pseudo-ideology of pure economism on the one side and the obstinate defence of the bastion of the welfare state on the other.

The British sociologist and political scientist Anthony Giddens, Director of the London School of Economics, took this polarization as the starting-point for his reflections on the possibility of a politics 'beyond left and right', which he published in 1996. According to Giddens, in a world in which the foundations of industrial society are continually being put in question by ever widening, ever accelerating global developments, politicians of all camps fall into the same trap: namely, the temptation of re-ideologization. On the right, philosophical conservatism is replaced by the philosophy of the free market. The conviction that there are traditions on which the future can be built is abandoned as an unnecessary encumbrance to progress, and all is staked on the ideology of global competition. Conservatism used to say: 'Things were nice as they were yesterday.' The free market's cold reply is: 'Just watch where it gets you.' At the same time the free market denies certain relationships which conservatism used to take as central – the relationship between economic policy and social policy, for instance, or between economic forces, ecology and the labour market. Market liberalism also denied the need for an alternative to economism itself, failing to understand that a country cannot be governed according to the dictates of business management alone.

On the other side, large swathes of opinion on the left no longer stand for progress and development but for passivity and defensiveness. Crises make for conservatism. Why are yesterday's progressives today's most stubborn resisters to new ideas? There is no way back to a traditional policy of redistribution. Even in Sweden, the archetypal social democratic country, Prime Minister Persson radically rejected any centralized management of the economy and subjected all welfare benefits to the test of justification. Parties of social democratic inclination which won elections in their countries in the 1990s, such as Clinton's Democratic Party in 1992 and Tony Blair's Labour Party in 1997, have all abandoned once and for all the tax-and-spend policies of the 1970s. The electors demand an alternative to free market dogma but have no desire to return to a form of state-controlled social democracy. It is not only the force of globalization that demands the modernization of our institutions and political programmes, but, to no less an extent, changes in patterns of employment, in values and in demographic and social structures. Can the social democratic parties of Europe unite to compose a new scenario for social and economic renewal, a new, concrete vision of how we want to live tomorrow? What ought the state to regulate – indeed, what can it regulate? How can economic, environmental and employment policies be reconciled? How can innovation be combined with justice?

In the face of the electoral successes of social democratic parties in the whole of Europe and the evident incapacity of free market reforms and solutions to resolve the situation, even Ralf Dahrendorf has gone back to some extent – as though confessing to a youthful indiscretion – on his pronouncement of 'the end of the social democratic century'. The renewal of the social democratic model beyond the categories of 'left' and 'right' is an international trend that takes account of realities that have been present for a long while. One such reality is the rediscovery of the value of co-operation and consensus. When in 1997 the attacks in Germany against the tendency towards consensus were still at their height, on the international scene the debate was beginning to go the other way. At an OECD meeting in 1996 the Nether-lands Minister of Social Affairs received a great deal of applause for his presentation of a 'consensus model' in a paper called 'Welfare State in Transition'. Until a few years ago the attitude still prevailed that negotiations would get one nowhere. Today, such solutions are regarded once again as successes. No single academic, political or social group can claim sole credit for this state of affairs – it is being promoted by rational thinkers and pragmatists of all parties and all countries. The international debate on the 'investor state', which mirrors this trend, is proof of the growing awareness that the question 'More state control or less?' did not get to the heart of the matter.

In an interview with the *Wirtschaftswoche* on 6 June 1996, Tony Blair defined the investor state thus:

> At the present time governments should not attempt to control their economies. The role of government today should be to pre-pare people and industry for change in key areas such as educa-tion and training, technology, infrastructure and help for small businesses. We do not want to show ourselves to be cleverer than the market. Rather, the state should act as a catalyst.

As Blair sees it, a 'stakeholder society' guarantees equality of opportunity. Only in this way can a society emerge that is ambi-tious without being selfish. Many see this as the hated com-promise of the left with the forces of the free market. But if we recall the original meaning of flexibility, it becomes clear that this is basically an emancipating conception of politics, in which the ability to adapt smoothly to changed conditions, while at the same time maintaining security and stability, is to be encouraged. The question is not so much what do we have to give up, but rather, what do we retain? – to which the answer is: the sense of a community in which people feel secure, confident that they can face the future together.

Popular analyses that set out to lay down the *only* macroeconomic framework and the *only* organizational form of the welfare state that is viable are making a fundamental error. Beneath the surface of globalization there lies a world that will accommodate the most varied forms of capitalism. In December 1997 *Time* magazine carried an article headed: 'Pathfinders: Can the Europeans build a Middle Road between Uncaring Capitalism and the Costly Welfare State?' The Europeans had set out, according to the article, to find ways of reducing unemployment and developing a new competitive edge without undermining the foundations of the welfare state. The path led, the article went on, to a 'durable' welfare state based on a new allocation of responsibilities between the state, the employers and the people.

In a number of countries of the European Union the author of the article found indications of how the Europeans were contriving to bring this about and what instruments they were employing. In Germany he was struck by the worker-oriented reorganization model of Volkswagen, an example of the key function of negotiated settlements in the processes of economic modernization. In Denmark, where all young people between the ages of 18 and 25 are offered initial training or a job, and are compelled to accept the offer, he saw new forms of co-operation between the unemployed, firms and employment agencies. The third way between the traditional welfare state and a free market economy thus takes a variety of forms, and experiments are still going on.

In Germany there is still ill-feeling towards the state for handing over responsibility from itself to its citizens. Freedom – guaranteed by the state – is defined in passive terms as freedom from unemployment, freedom from poverty, freedom from the consequences of disability. This conception of the state as 100 per cent responsible for its citizens from the cradle to the grave is not only a relic of the days of the German Democratic Republic – it is increasingly being recognized that it is a model that works only in fine weather. The mechanisms that were set up to convert more and more of the individual's scope for making his own decisions into the exercise of regimented standards and administrative regulations have become bureaucratic monsters. Since 1950 the number of public servants has grown five times as fast as that of the population as a whole, and it will not be long before the spectre of the cost of pensions returns to haunt the national exchequer. The number of rules and regulations has been steadily rising, and the recent spate of privatizations and attempts at deregulation has had no effect. Indeed, all these measures only resulted in a fresh flood of re-regulation statutes and new procedures.

A general distrust of material success and independence has grown up which has become an established feature of the modern German character – a kind of institutionalized rejection of responsibility. A large proportion of German university graduates still prefer a career in public administration or industrial management to joining the ranks of the self-employed. In 1996 some 54 per cent of graduates found their way into the public service sector. Only in the younger age groups have there been recent signs of a change in this trend.

Whilst more and more private individuals play the stock market, setting out to make money in dubious derivatives under high-risk conditions, management careers requiring long-term commitment enjoy little popularity. There is no contradiction in this. Whereas the welfare state has a monopoly of long-term security and has, as it were, nationalized the individual's responsibility for large segments of his life, the philosophy of 'Get in quick, get out quick' offers some kind of compensation. Klaus von Dohnanyi once observed: 'The Germans see the welfare state as the nation. There is nothing of substance apart from the successful welfare state which unites them in patriotic pride.' They are welfare state patriots.

When in June 1948 General Lucius Clay, commander of the American occupation troops in Berlin after the Second World War, accused Ludwig Erhard of changing the rationing regulations without permission, Erhard retorted, in words that have gone down in history: 'I haven't changed the regulations – I've abolished them.'

Things are not that easy today. We are facing the challenge of how to change from a form of 'state socialism' to a new model of the welfare state. This requires new aims in welfare policy – more individual responsibility and readiness to take risks, and a proactive state. The foundations are in place.

On the one hand, it is true to say that in the German welfare state a readiness to takes risks was always less in evidence than in other countries. On the other hand, in Germany too, people find ways of circumventing official regulations when they feel that the state is breathing down their necks and preventing them from exercising their own initiative. Where parties, unions and other associations are concerned we can see this in phenomena such as moonlighting, tax evasion and a massive 'voting with their feet'. There has also been a resistance on the part of a growing number of owners of small and medium-sized businesses to compulsory membership of trade associations and chambers of commerce. In short, the situation on the ground is coming to outweigh the influence of institutions and their political programmes.

In the future the state will have to be seen as the head office of a corporation, the function of which is less to intervene directly than to coax its members, through organizational changes and modifications, to achieve the highest possible degree of economic and social productivity. Parallels with the reorganization of industrial complexes and service industries are obvious. What Henry Ford was able to achieve on the production line with an army of book-keepers is today assembled by a series of flexible profit centres. Decentralized enterprises with virtually no hierarchy constitute an innovative avant-garde. What used to be centrally and authoritatively administered in the welfare state can in the future only be contained within a more flexible network of control systems. Division of labour, decentralization and internationalization all demand an ever-increasing degree of joint responsibility on the part of employees – which is equally true of their role as citizens.

In 1997 the OECD demanded strong political leadership in order to convince people of the need for reforms and to gain their agreement to a new balance between rights and obligations. Social security has a particular role to play in this, according to the report; it must be organized in such a way that people are encouraged and enabled to take risks, and to react in a flexible way to changes in their economic environment.

For this purpose we need a 'policy for second chances'. It is not only those who, pampered by the benefits of the welfare state, have lost the sense of personal initiative, who have grown to be afraid of taking risks, but also those who find it difficult to recover from even the slightest of setbacks. The state must ensure that employers and employees alike, expert advisers and business managers, are in a position to stand up to competitive pressures. Companies are exposed to international competition and have to play by its rules. On the other side they are also confronted by national policies which are working towards uniformity and standardization. If the welfare state is to be preserved, national regulations must be made more flexible and be supplemented, above all at the European level, by new instruments of negotiation aimed at achieving a balance of interests. The system of local wage agreements, for example, was instituted in order to establish fair competitive conditions over the country as a whole. In future, these agreements will have to offer more room for manoeuvre, so that individual strategies can be adopted to deal with international competition.

This also applies to social systems. In the face of changed preferences in modes of cohabitation, new forms of family unit and changes in patterns of employment, social policy must abandon its normative conceptions and draw up a new framework within which self-determination, personal responsibility and security are all mutually compatible. More individual responsibility on the part of workers, companies and government departments is necessary in order to be reliable, innovative and flexible when confronted with new and unpredictable developments. From training to acquiring employment, from health provision to retirement pensions – in every field the element of individual responsibility must be strengthened if our social system is to move with the times in an increasingly decentralized information society. There will no more central control monopolies, but fair regulatory systems for changing competitive conditions and individual challenges: no more traditional standardization in the pensions and welfare systems, but a new context of consensus and solidarity. The state must not pursue a bureaucratic policy of egalitarianism in the efficient wealth-producing population, nor must it become the mere apologist for the market to the genuinely disadvantaged but the guarantor of a fair balance between the givers and the takers as a precondition for solidarity.

Our ideal is that of a proactive state, a state that makes things possible. The question facing us is: do we want equality at the end or equality at the beginning, i.e. equality of opportunity? We have reached a dead end with the policy of handing out what the norm said people were entitled to, based on the calculations and private influence of lobby groups but not on the interests of those who were really in need of help. We must assist people to get what they most need in each situation in which they find themselves – and in the majority of cases, according to the experience of many communities, this is not a welfare cheque but a proper job. Social policy also has to justify itself in economic terms, which means modernization under conditions of globalization.

We need economically viable ideas at the heart of our social and welfare policies. In the social market economy an efficient social policy and a socially responsible economic policy are two sides of the same coin. Economic efficiency has its roots in human capital and properly functioning social institutions, whereas a badly functioning economy will hinder social progress and lead to increased polarization and social stress.

The pendulum is about to swing towards a new social democratic model. At the heart of this model lies the vision that people want to be reunited under a single idea, a vision of how we want to live tomorrow. This vision is not to be confused with an ideology. It is to be interpreted completely pragmatically. If you are prepared, we say, to take your life in your own hands, we will put plans before you which are worth while putting into practice – and we will act as a safety net. If one says that it must be made worth while to work rather than to receive welfare hand-outs, it would be invidious simply to reduce these hand-outs. That would spell not the creation of opportunities for work, but their destruction. It would be more sensible and more honest to introduce at long last the concept of topping-up minimal incomes. Any journalist can ring up his paper's office and discover how difficult it to find a reliable delivery man for a low wage. Thus, in spite of the crisis surrounding the availability of apprenticeships, many workshops report that they cannot find school leavers prepared to take up training. It is a situation that gives much food for thought.

A mentality has developed that regards it at best as superfluous, and at worst as pointless, to roll up one's sleeves. We need to send out a clear signal: make an effort, and we will give you the money so that you can save on our behalf by preferring to take a job to collecting a weekly benefit cheque. To cut the funds available for a proactive employment policy is an unimaginative solution and is itself, according to the Federal Labour Office in Nuremberg, partly responsible for the unemployment situation. Subsidized part-term work, flexible working, incentives for the employment of the long-term unemployed in successful industries and a programme of further education and training geared to the demands of a changed society – such are some of the possibilities open to us.

We must have recourse to instruments which encourage self-help, personal initiative and enterprise, and support for those with the determination to take up the challenge. It is easy just to refer to the consequences of globalization. More sensible would be to prepare people for the competition that innovation is going to bring with it. If we are to break down the obstacles that have been raised against innovation, we must offer venture capital to those with a gift for invention and a willingness to put their careers on the line.

It would be equally wrong for us to let pushy operators elbow their way to the top, bank on the winners, and be prepared to watch the weaker brethren go to the wall. A more sensible procedure would be to promote independence and enterprise as alternatives for everybody. In the Netherlands social workers are paid according to how many young people they find regular jobs for. We cannot go on simply subsidizing. No longer can we afford just to subsidize welfare efforts – we must also check success rates and reward efficiency. Measures aimed at removing polarization in business, in the labour market and in society cannot be allowed any longer to peter out in distributive processes but must be made to enable people to acquire higher skills and a greater degree of responsibility. Everybody must be given the chance to make a fortune – but we cannot guarantee that it will happen.

We need a radical pragmatic policy for the middle ground in society which does not regard public spirit and economic freedom as conflicting forces, but reunites them as complementary interests. The safeguards that such a policy offers will not be the old ones. Nobody today can be sure of spending their whole life working at a lathe or sitting at a desk. No one can even be certain that on the basis of a single qualification it will be possible to stay all one's life doing one and the same kind of job. The areas in which the state will be able to intervene in the lives of its citizens and take over their responsibilities will be very restricted. This is as it should be. People do not want the state constantly breathing down their necks but want to have it on hand in case of need. They want a state that takes the question of internal security seriously, one which does not get tied up in a mass of red tape at the slightest provocation but which at the same time can cordon off whole areas of a city, the station forecourt, parks and public buildings at certain times of the day.

Anybody who turns these matters over in their mind will have no difficulty in finding proactive policies to deal with all the problems that confront us, policies to be put into practice by a proactive state that will overcome our present state of paralysis. A proactive economic policy, for instance, will be concerned to encourage independence and the creation of new businesses where capital markets are reluctant to invest, and to enable medium-sized businesses to face the challenges of globalization. In the *Länder* that made up the former GDR we can see what happens when old instruments are employed to deal with new problems, both in the economic field and in the field of employment. The provision of risk capital is becoming an ever more important instrument. German bankruptcy law is also in urgent need of revision.

Let us take another area. In a proactive ecological policy the aim will be to engage the technological potentials and the ingenuity of the engineers directly in the production of a strategy for the protection of the environment, instead of bureaucratizing the procedures of conservation and leaving the level of technological development where it is. We have reached the point where it no longer appears reasonable to spend huge sums of money in trying to remove the final 2 per cent of toxic emissions in our country when it is possible to develop integrated environment technologies capable of being exported and employed in improving conditions in the environment worldwide.

With the same matter-of-course mentality with which we introduced works safety measures into our production procedures, making them a trademark of our operations and exporting them as proof of the quality of our goods, we must now integrate long-term reliability and error-friendliness. We cannot turn our backs on the industrial society and its dependence on natural resources.

This is also well known to the scientists in the Wuppertal Institute, who, with their so-called 'factor of four', have raised the question, not by chance, of productivity and its relationship to long-termism. The question is not whether natural resources will one day be exhausted but how this will happen. Even the German Confederation of Industries is talking today of long-termism, and the subject has also become part of the curriculum in courses in engineering in our universities. The challenges of long-term growth are principally technological challenges. An ecology policy administered by bureaucrats is an anachronism. It leaves no room for the selection of procedures and structures that prove in the end to be the most durable. Administrative rules may on occasion prove a useful corrective, but that is not to be confused with the idea that bureaucracies produce the best results. The availability of a mass of statutes and regulations will not make the world an ecologically more friendly place.

A striking image invented by the Swedes compared social security to a trampoline, on which those who have fallen out of the job market can bounce back and land on their feet. Every socio-political instrument has its economic and employment-policy aspect. The state must not only balance the negative aspects of one 'sub-system' – economic, social, political – against the others, or prevent such aspects appearing, but also achieve the highest possible degree of integration between the systems. The social system, for instance, must be so conceived that it permits and encourages a return to active work and the restoration of individual initiative. A new balance between individual rights and obligations must be evolved. At the same time a proactive state must show more confidence in its citizens and allow them to shoulder more responsibilities. This does not mean that the state is turning its back on its own obligations. Quite the contrary. The challenge is to evolve a new control model which will require far more creativity and readiness to innovate, together with a long-term view of future political development, than the old, prescriptive model.

This becomes all the clearer when one realizes that even in the most fundamental areas of the state's activity there will be no avoiding the need for new conceptions. Take the question of the law. Over recent years the law has shown itself unable to prevent an increase in conflict situations and litigation. The number of civil actions in Germany in courts of first instance rose from 1.3 million in 1980 to almost 2.2 million in 1995, and is still rising. The courts are being swamped by legal actions of one kind or another, many of them over trivialities. Large sectors of public life have become governed by legal procedures. It has become increasingly difficult for individual citizens to recognize what their rights and duties are and to balance these rights and duties against those of others. A flood of new prescriptive rules and regulations is descending on us. In 1949–50 the Federal Statute Book comprised 825 pages. By 1994 Part One of the Statute Book had swollen to 4,000 pages and three volumes, a body of legislation that even professional lawyers have difficulty in handling. And besides this there is the legislation produced by the sixteen individual *Länder* and by the European Union.

This increase in the number of official regulations has had the effect of increasing the individual's willingness to take matters to court. There is hardly a television channel in the country today that does not have its consumer programme, in which the public air their complaints and seek redress for alleged injustices. An impenetrable jungle of laws and statutes leads to a deluge of litigation and inscrutable legal decisions. More and more people seem to find satisfaction in devising ever more determined or devious ways of asserting and defending their alleged rights in courts of law. Besides this, defaulting debtors have long discovered that lengthy legal proceedings are a cheap way of getting credit, because cases can drag on for anything up to two years.

Legal verdicts themselves are also becoming less and less relevant, often taking so long to be delivered that they become meaningless. And because they are based solely on the facts pertaining to the formal presentation of the case, they ignore the real causes of the dispute, such as personal insults and old grudges, or a demand for emotional redress. In such circumstances legal judgements do not bring about peace. Minor subjects of disagreement may be settled but the legal battles continue. The state is blamed for private offences. In May 1998 a pensioner shot a judge in a fit of paranoia because he felt unfairly treated by a legal system against which he himself had levelled one charge after another.

Nor does the 'complaints mentality' shrink from involving the highest court in the land. The Federal Constitutional Court is forced into the role of legislator whenever politicians have proved incapable of arriving at a decision. When the *Länder* in the south of the country brought a case alleging an unfair allocation of funds between the federal government and the *Länder*, on the question of ante-natal clinics and the deployment of German troops abroad;

or even in the matter of the orthography of the German language
– in all such cases the supreme court was relegated to the role of
an agency called in to complete a task that the politicians had
shown themselves incapable of mastering.

Nor do the various arbitration courts command much respect
from the population as a whole – which is no surprise, given the
state of the nation's politics. Some 5,000 complaints a year are
lodged with the Constitutional Court by citizens who consider
that their rights have been infringed by public authorities, but
90 per cent of these are turned down at the preliminary stage on
the grounds of insufficient evidence, and only 1 per cent are successful. Polls conducted in 1995 showed that the high respect
in which the Constitutional Court used to be held has fallen in
recent years by 10 per cent to a mere 40 per cent.

A further cause of the Court's loss of esteem has been the
outspoken attacks on it by political parties which were forced to
see the exercise of their power to rule – or mis-rule – criticized
and reviewed. The issue of a minimum wage is a case in point.
Neighbours who go to court over the compost heap on the border
between their gardens, a gigantic increase in the cases coming
before the Administration Court – all this shows that a mentality
has grown up that is opposed to consensus and compromise even
at the lowest level. Politics and the law, moreover, have tolerated
this transfer of responsibility from the bottom to the top, and not
infrequently encouraged it. A proactive state would be entitled
to say to its citizens: 'Pull yourselves together!'

In the United States steps have been taken to counter such
conflicts of interest, which were spiralling out of control and
sometimes took on bizarre forms. There, the traditional court
hearing is only one of a number of ways of resolving conflicts.
From a wide range of conciliation procedures the warring parties
can select the one that seems to them the most appropriate. It is
even possible to conduct proceedings before a mock jury so as to
assess more realistically one's chances of success. This procedure
has in the meantime become so firmly established in the legal
system that people talk in everyday conversation no longer of an
'alternative' settlement but of an 'appropriate' settlement. Every
state in the union now has legal rules, or at least local regulations, which provide for such procedures.

And not only in the courts are conflicts now being settled
by consensus: authorities too are using the new instruments to

involve the participation of the citizens. Quite incidentally, all this led to a boom in the seeking of legal advice: a whole area of activity which had hitherto lived on the back of the mass of lawsuits (and still does in Germany) began to change its approach because the state had changed the guidelines, unable and unwilling to allow its citizens to seek continual recourse to the courts without rhyme or reason.

The *Land* of North-Rhine-Westphalia proposed a new legal procedure. This would entail compulsory conciliation proceedings which, in cases where the financial consideration at issue does not exceed 1,500 marks, would have to be concluded before the matter could be referred to the courts. Only after having tried to settle by conciliation would one be permitted to sue. The North-Rhine-Westphalian Ministry of Justice has calculated that in the country as a whole some 280,000 potential litigants could be made to settle their differences by this means.

Experts see chances to extend this conciliation process. It could be used, for example, in house-building disputes, in conflicts over contracts between main contractors and self-employed tradesmen, in arguments with architects and landlords, or in settling negligence claims against doctors. Clarification of the facts of the case could take place away from the formal atmosphere of the courtroom. Whereas judges must be at pains to retain their power of passing judgement, mediators could resolve the dispute in discussions. Mediators might be attorneys, retired judges or even trained jurymen. Judgements could naturally be challenged, and all the other courses of legal action would still be open.

One could compare the situation with the wearing of seat-belts in cars. Only when it was made compulsory did people realize the value of the measure. We seem to have to be forced to change our modes of thought if we are to stop ourselves turning into a society of grumblers. It is a process, moreover, that must start in school. The increasing violence in our schools is a sign of the brutalization of society, a warning that society is in danger of losing the ability to resolve its conflicts. The USA took almost 20 years to change its attitude towards the legal system and is now also trying out new ideas in the field of internal security. We have to time to lose.

We need a similar initiative in the area of internal security. Is it possible to revive local government without a feeling of security and responsibility? Not unless the people can be galvanized into assuming responsibility for their own local affairs. An important element in the conception of a proactive state is thus the campaign against crime and its causes. Only when people clearly see that the state is out to protect them and their property from attack and defend their long-term interests against organized crime will they have confidence in the state and be prepared to play an active part in the affairs of the community. 'Tough on crime and tough on the causes of crime' – this must be our philosophy. In Denmark juvenile crime is being successfully tackled by punishing offenders immediately but at the same time making the parents face their responsibilities by involving the whole family in the process of reintegration into the community.

These are, of course, only individual aspects of the problem. The range of issues stretches from a fair taxation policy to the avoidance of imprudent government spending. And it can be extended in the field of government spending from the system of special allowances to public sector workers – which we should replace by offering better chances of promotion – down to the abolition of the three-stage wage structure based on the acquisition of formal qualifications. We can accept privileges for special groups on political grounds, if that is what society wants. But conditions in the public sector are such as to make that hardly possible. The constantly growing number of local authorities that are experimenting with new organizational models, setting out to be more customer-friendly and offer a better service, and able to point to considerable motivational success, shows the extent of the needs of local authorities and the public sector as a whole for more room to manoeuvre and a greater degree of individual accountability.

I am well aware that proactive policies that cannot contemplate a retreat from the principle of individual responsibility will come into conflict with people and organizations whose existence appears to be based on the principle of an institutionalized refusal to accept responsibility. Such people would be at their happiest as public officials without a public, or as doctors and administrators in the best-equipped hospitals but without patients, or as teachers in schools with no pupils – even as business managers for whom customers are disruptive elements, and who ignore their dependence on subsidies, possibly producing some of the best products that money can buy – but for non-existent markets.

On the subject of the relationship between the individual and the state I take my stand on one overriding principle. Only a proactive state can expect of its citizens the loyalty that finds its natural outlet in the renewed call for a new sense of community. The proactive state is a partner in the individual's journey through life, not a teacher or a leader. It can offer tailor-made plans to help people back into independent careers in times of crisis, financed by their own honest efforts. It would be a big mistake to overlook the fact that an individual's social status depends to a large extent on his job. It is a characteristic of industrial societies that a person's job is one of the ways of defining his place in that society.

Proactive policies require, *inter alia*, a greater degree of transparency in the financing of the state and its welfare provisions, together with enhanced scope for individual responsibility and private financial provision. The welfare state does not allow employees enough freedom to make their own social security arrangements. The burden of tax deductions and welfare contributions has reached grotesque proportions – this is the common denominator of all diagnoses of the crisis in which the welfare state and the labour market find themselves. People have no objection to paying taxes for education, for the police, for health insurance and for the public infrastructure. But they do object to paying for political failure.

Since 1991 real labour costs (price adjusted) have risen over the country as a whole by 11.3 per cent and wages (gross) by 7 per cent. But according to calculations by bodies as different as the German Trades Union Congress and the Institute for German Industry and Commerce, price-adjusted net earnings in the former West Germany actually fell by 2 per cent in 1997. In the same year, as a result, purchasing power per employee fell below the level of 1980.

This development had further consequences. In 1998, owing to changes in the pension insurance scheme that followed the reform of the pensions system, falling or stagnating net earnings were reflected for the first time in pensions increases below the rate of inflation. But part of the blame for the fall in net earnings lay with the rise in pensions contributions. How is an employee expected to understand this state of affairs?

There is no doubt that these developments disadvantaged employees. But there can also be no doubt that they encouraged firms neither to invest in new jobs nor to increase consumption and stimulate demand. True, according to the Bundesbank in its business report for 1997, wage unit costs have fallen appreciably. But the vital consideration in this reluctance to take on more workers is that in the former West Germany the hourly rate is now almost 9 per cent higher than it was in 1991. If workers have not noticed this, then it is because the ever-increasing deductions for tax and social security are driving an ever thicker wedge between the labour costs that employers have to bear and the wages that they pay out. On the one hand the increase in taxes and welfare contributions could not be completely offset by wage reductions, while on the other hand gross wage increases could not under these circumstances be converted into consumption and domestic demand. As long as rising wages led to increased purchasing power, the policy of urging ever greater productivity could be said to work. But today there is no longer any connection between the two. The cost of taxes and welfare contributions puts a brake on consumer demand and at the same time prevents employers from investing in jobs.

In the last two years there has been a change in the terminology employed in public discussions on these issues. People used to talk about 'subsidiary costs'; now they refer to them as 'wage-added costs'. Skilled workers in Germany enjoy their share of praise, and even our bitterest rivals in world markets concede that nowhere in the world are there to be found better trained workers. Yet almost every day since 1995 these workers have been reading in the papers that they are too expensive compared with workers in other countries, and that they should give up working overtime for the benefit of the unemployed – although, according to Chancellor Kohl, they were already enjoying the conditions of a 'holiday camp'. They were told to tighten their belts, which were already in the last hole. They cannot understand why they are said to be too expensive – an understandable reaction when they look at the net wage on their pay slip. Employers, however, calculate on the basis of gross wages and added costs, and look at nothing else. Meanwhile, 84 per cent of workers have come to the conclusion that taxes and welfare deductions are responsible for the economic crisis.

At the end of 1997 a television documentary called 'How to take the workers for a ride' met with horrified reactions. A group of typical German workers was invited into the studio and shown the yawning gap that had opened up between their gross earnings and their take-home pay. An example was given of a skilled worker in a machine tool factory, married, with two children. The employer's gross wage costs, including social security contributions, amounted to 7,974 marks. After deducting income tax and the social security contributions of employer and employee, the latter was left with take-home pay of 3,897 marks, i.e. roughly half what he 'cost' his employer – 48.9 per cent, to be exact.

But this is not the end of the story. A man on average earnings with a family to support faces additional taxes on almost 100 per cent of his income – value-added tax, duty on alcohol and petrol and so on, which are dismissed as 'indirect taxes'. Of the price of a litre of petrol, 80 per cent goes in duty, and even incidental expenses in the home contain almost 25 per cent tax. Even when the family goes out for a meal at a not exorbitant cost of 70 marks, 11.20 marks go to the exchequer. Of the price of a crate of beer, 4 marks go in duty.

All this may sound like hair-splitting. But one cannot avoid a barrage of statistics if one is to calculate the real extent of the tax and social security burden that the average worker has to bear. One needs data from the payroll office, the figures on the pay slip, information from the finance director and the bank manager, advice from tax advisers and so on. This concerns all of us. Who, for example, knows for certain what is his top tax bracket?

A lack of transparency is itself one of the scandals of our tax system. But there is an even worse scandal. Our average worker ultimately retains a mere 34.3 per cent as an 'absolute net sum' after the deduction of all direct and indirect taxes, all social security contributions and so on. What he gets back in child allowance, house purchase allowance, tax repayments and the like had already been deducted. Such a situation prevails in almost every German household, and all the experts agree on the basic findings.

Look, by contrast, at the situation in the United States. Here, a worker retains an 'absolute net sum' of over 60 per cent. In Japan the figure is only slightly lower. Thirty years ago, in the days of Ludwig Erhard, the average worker paid 10 per cent in direct tax and a further 10 per cent of his gross wages for social security. The rest he could save towards building a house – seen today, incidentally, as an inherited asset on the basis of which critics of the affluent society try to make out that Germany has never had it so good. In 1997 various models for tax cuts were discussed, including a plan that failed to get through the Bundesrat. But for the skilled worker who is hardly able to build up capital and uses every penny to satisfy the needs of himself and his family, only one tangible result emerged from these discussions – an increase of 1 per cent in value-added tax, the tax that strikes the hardest.

Reductions in overtime working? Short-time working without loss of wages? Many see such proposals as holding the answer to the problem of unemployment, but there is a good deal of evidence to show that high taxation is driving people increasingly into moonlighting and bogus self-employment. Overtime is a built-in factor in earnings. There is as yet no empirical evidence to confirm it, but some experts are of the opinion that as a result of a reduction in the working week in the Volkswagen factory in Wolfsburg to 28.5 hours – with a corresponding reduction in wages – the incidence of moonlighting in the Wolfsburg area has gone up. According to calculations made by the local trades association in the nearby town of Gifhorn, estates are springing up in the outlying rural areas where there is not a single building, apart from the church, that has not been built with the help of moonlighters, and every third of these 'helpers' is a Volkswagen employee. Many houses, it is said, would not have been built at all but for moonlighters.

Few have any guilty feelings about this. To live in one's own four walls is the most important contribution one can make towards securing one's future. But in this case it is only made possible by adopting unlawful labour practices. A skilled worker who wants to buy a house, let alone build from scratch, has to invest all his saving – and that, moreover, in a situation that can no longer guarantee permanent employment. The taboo that used to hang over moonlighting seems to have been broken. It has become a fixed part of our gross domestic product, and for the individual, apparently, a kind of self-defence against the demands made by the welfare state.

As long as no fundamental changes are made in the tax and insurance contributions burden for middle-income groups, any plans for an increase in personal provision for one's own social security, or for participation in the process of wealth-creation, are pointless. Employees are left with no room to exercise their own sense of responsibility, nor are they asked for their views.

The only contribution to solidarity and fairness they are allowed to make takes the form of deductions. They lose all sense of personal accountability, swamped by a society governed by delegations and committees. There is a growing tendency to try and get as much as possible out of one's insurance policies by making false claims, or to employ various tricks to get out of paying income tax. If one kept strictly within the law, one would find that there are many things one could no longer afford. Such a situation masks the real nature of the problem.

At the same time the plausibility of the debate over 'the end of the period of restraint' on the part of the workers and their unions also has to be tested against the background of the gap between gross earnings and take-home pay. On the one hand the wage restraint exercised by workers and unions in the second half of the 1990s has largely been abandoned. The needs of the federal treasury and of the social security system have led to higher taxes and welfare contributions; this in turn has a negative effect on employment, the labour market gets into difficulties, the costs of welfare rise etc., etc. Responsible union leaders who stood up in the 1990s for moderate wage demands are in danger of being slated by fellow delegates because at grass-roots level the situation is not acceptable – a warning signal not to threaten the unions' influence.

If an employer pays a married couple with two children an extra 100 marks, the couple is left after deductions with just 43,13 marks to spend. Nevertheless in 1996 the Germans managed to save 11.6 per cent of their net incomes, which means that another 5 marks was taken from the imaginary wage rise. And from the remaining 38,13 marks, the German economy derives only limited benefit, for strictly speaking one should deduct the 70 billion marks that are spent annually on holidays abroad, and, if one were to take it to extremes, the cost of imported goods and services whose net product lies outside the country – 10.9 per cent of the average income goes on the purchase of foreign goods. So at the end what is left from the 100-mark pay rise is the princely sum of 27,23 marks to spend in the home market.

In addition, we need to realize that from the employer's point of view a 100-mark pay rise for an employee actually costs him 121 marks, since he has his own contribution to make to social security costs. As a result, labour costs amount to four times the additionally created domestic demand. We must therefore find acceptable ways of reducing the gap between labour costs and net wages. This would stimulate consumption and create jobs. In his programme 'One Nation Society', Tony Blair redefined, almost in passing, an age-old social democratic principle, namely that justice means allowing every man to retain the lion's share of what he has produced by his own efforts.

Reference to the cost of German reunification, in particular in the area of social security, is relevant, but by itself it does not advance the argument. The financing of public expenditure through tax revenue has always been a basic feature of social democratic policies, and it could be the first important step along the road to a wider involvement of all groups in society in the financing of the welfare state. But this must not be allowed to develop, in the long term, into a position where costs financed by contributions are converted into costs financed by taxation – robbing Peter to pay Paul, in other words. Budgetary and other technical solutions which have a prompt effect will need to be supplemented by structural reforms in public administration and in both the taxation and welfare systems, which will put a brake on the rise in costs over the medium term.

There have been occasions when the craziness of the entire system has become blindingly obvious. One was in May 1998, when Horst Seehofer, Federal Minister of Health, addressed the annual meeting of the German Medical Association in Cologne and announced that a sharp rise in doctors' fees was fully justified. Seehofer knew where the money would have to come from – from rises in the dues of the medical insurance companies. At the same meeting the 250 delegates called for the benefits paid out by these companies to be reduced. This is more than a joke – it is a description of a madhouse. The negotiating parties which since the 1970s have shared responsibility for the increase in added costs arising from the wage agreements they concluded can no longer escape their share of blame for such a hair-raising state of affairs.

The severest test facing the SPD government in Germany is in the field of taxation policy. The acceptability of a tax system depends on two factors. The first is the clarity and transparency of the regulations; the second is the uses to which the money is put and the credibility of government policy. Tax reform in these terms, simply and cogently expressed, corresponds to what people find sensible and reasonable, and is not really controversial. To make tax rates at the upper end of the scale match what is actually paid out, after taking account of all the allowances claimed and tax evasion dodges employed, is simply common sense. Equally sensible is to reduce the rate of taxation for those in the lower ranges, so as to increase purchasing power, offer incentives to take up productive work and make moonlighting less lucrative. To allow tax relief on investments in production and labour at the expense of capital investment would be the most rational policy imaginable. An increase in inheritance tax, on the other hand, could be defended on grounds of social justice.

But in reality no one can comprehend our present system. Nobody was able to follow the hair-splitting arguments put forward in the course of the debate on taxation policy and the reform of the welfare system in 1997 and 1998. The proposal to finance a 1 per cent reduction in wage-added costs by a 1 per cent increase in value-added tax provided enough food for thought. Today more than ever we must try to escape from such a situation. If it is true, as is said, that economic policy is first and foremost a matter of psychology, then it is particularly relevant to the psychological effects of a radical U-turn in the field of taxation.

Revenue from taxation is declining with each successive estimate: the most productive sources of income are either growing sluggishly, stagnating or shrinking. According to figures for the middle of 1998 the three sources that together make up around 70 per cent of the total tax revenue – turnover tax, income tax and duty on mineral oil – grew by a mere 0.4 per cent, and that figure was reached only because turnover tax yielded around 1.9 per cent more than in the previous year. Not for the first time did the so-called experts get it spectacularly wrong – in 1995 they had miscalculated by more than 5 billion marks.

It was not that federal and provincial experts, those of the Bundesbank, the economic research institutes and other organizations, and the statisticians, had all forgotten how to count – they were victims of a new development. One can no longer assume that economic growth brings in additional revenue. Taxes have ceased to be linked to growth, as has the labour market. Since 1995 tax revenue has been declining: up to that point statisticians had always rounded their calculations upwards. Today we await their forecasts in fear and trembling, especially those working in local and provincial government. Between 1991 and 1997, as a result of changes in taxation law, the federal exchequer received a total of 71.9 billion marks, while the *Länder* and local authorities had to accept losses totalling 13 billion marks.

A considerable dent has been made in tax revenues by the rapid drop in income tax. Income tax regulations change from one year to the next. There has been a perpetual process of plugging loopholes, placating particular groups of taxpayers and satisfying sectional interests, but no overriding concept. Over a mere five-year period revenue from income tax fell from 41.5 billion marks (1992) to little more than a tenth of this (4.5 billion) in 1997. The missing sum roughly corresponds to the insurance tax plus tobacco and alcohol duties for 1997. But for the Germans' thirst and addiction to cigarettes, the country's finances would collapse.

The real heart of the problem is an absurd and impenetrable taxation system which no one can understand. During Theo Waigel's term of office as Finance Minister the jungle of regulations became even more impenetrable. Even the simple subject of motor vehicle tax has become a mystery. President Roman Herzog had harsh words for the judiciary when he accused it of passing over-subtle judgements and thereby itself contributing to the confusion. 'If a person can make something more complicated,' said Herzog, 'he can also make it simpler again.'

A simple, intelligible system of taxation, like welfare and employment policies, can encourage people to develop a sense of public responsibility. As things stand, well-to-do taxpayers are spending hours on calculating their allowances and deductions. The result is that tax is paid on only half of all incomes. Tax exiles deprive the exchequer of billions of marks, and the viability of the German treasury depends on the willingness of neighbouring states such as Luxemburg to introduce taxation at source. This has alarming consequences for the country's finances. In the meantime the principle of progressive taxation has also been virtually abandoned as a result of reductions in direct and increases in indirect taxation, and in particular in the wake of cunningly devised tax-saving models which only take effect when a taxpayer is in the 45 per cent tax band.

Large companies are playing the same game. According to research carried out by a number of financial experts, in the thirty largest German joint stock companies tax on profits fell between 1989 and 1994 from 48 per cent to just below 24 per cent. Big companies are able to spread their profits according to where tax rates are at their lowest, and to employ various other stratagems such as switching production from one country to another, introducing internal settlements or founding finance houses – their tactics have become increasingly subtle over recent years. Smaller businesses, on the other hand, are not in a position to switch their profits: their share of the tax burden, measured by the European average, rose between 1980 and 1994 from 34 per cent to over 40 per cent.

A radical reform of the European tax system can only be successful if based on simple basic principles, not on highly complex systems. A simplification of the German taxation system is a precondition for the introduction of measures to curb European tax-dumping. This applies equally to the argument that the high tax rates in Germany are responsible for the lack of direct investment from abroad. Rainer Hübner set the record straight in an article in the journal *Capital* in August 1997. Whereas, he said, the industrial giants liked to depict themselves as the 'nation's paymasters', in reality the generous rules for calculating profits in Germany fully compensated for the advantage of lower American or even Dutch tax rates. Losses can be carried forward or carried back, and there are endless possibilities for deferment of payment. Tax loopholes make up 26 per cent of the total volume of company budgets – three times as much as in France or Italy. Although firms are again achieving returns on capital as high as they were at the beginning of the 1970s, the yield from corporation tax is stagnant – 29.5 billion marks in 1996, less than in the mid-1980s. Normally, however, foreign investors take their bearings from nominal tax rates. Low but 'honest', watertight rates, therefore, are the only way of making tax revenue calculable and at the same time facilitating investment.

Half the German population admits to being prepared to indulge in tax evasion. According to a survey conducted by the Institute for Socio-Economics in Cologne, 74 per cent feel that the government wastes so much of the taxpayers' money (70 billion marks a year), and companies avoid paying so much in welfare contributions, that it is not really morally reprehensible for individuals to do their own bit of tax-dodging. Asked what they would consider a 'gross breach' of the tax laws, 70 per cent replied: the way the government squandered the revenues it received from taxation; then followed the creation of bogus firms, the transfer of one's domicile abroad and the concealment of second sources of income. If the incidence of legal tax ruses grows, and the payment through taxation of a contribution towards public expenditure becomes a game of hide-and-seek, no one can be surprised that people avoid paying taxes. When, after a failed attempt at reforming the system, the political parties complain that a dentist pays less tax than a cleaner, the mass of the taxpayers can only raise a bitter laugh.

Governments and political parties have always kept their supporters happy with tax breaks of one kind or another. Taxation policy has been used to promote the interests of the family, to encourage the housebuilding programme and to stimulate investment or consumption. The various clauses of the regulations governing income tax and corporation tax reflect the political skirmishing over emergency budgetary provisions or tax loopholes. Thirty years ago the scientific advisory committee of the federal Finance Ministry demanded that the jungle of tax regulations be cleared away and tax rates radically reduced. But since that time, for every loophole that has been cleared at least one other has been legally opened. The basic question is how in a democratic society can freedom of action be guaranteed at all public levels? How can we secure capital for domestic economic projects when it will always find its way to international sources which offer high and quick returns? If Germany were to bring the nominal tax burden into line with the actual figure, the exchequer would not lose anything but the off-putting effect of being seen as a country of high taxation would disappear.

This becomes clear when one considers the possibility of a flat rate tax on all incomes – a spectre that haunts the taxation policies of all the parties. In 1994 total earnings for the whole of Germany amounted to 2,569 billion marks. In the same year 15.6 per cent of this was deducted for income tax, corporation tax and business tax. According to Thilo Sarrazin, an expert in taxation matters, the same amount could be raised by a flat rate tax of 20.5 per cent with a tax-free allowance of 15,000 marks per taxpayer, provided all sources of income were included. Lower income earners would pay far less tax, and the scale of the tax would remove the attraction of tax evasion and of the majority of tax-avoidance schemes. Although it is politically not feasible, the flat rate tax model does illustrate the basic argument that should be at the forefront of all discussion on tax reform, namely that if effective rate cuts are to be combined with high profitability, the basis on which the tax system rests must be comprehensively redefined.

The failure of all attempts at reform has two causes. One is that the political price to be paid for removing concessions was for all the parties too high, and the amount of energy needed to break up private sectional interests too great. Maybe what we require is a reversal of the burden of proof: all tax concessions would be radically withdrawn at the beginning, without exception, and those who maintained that they were entitled to such concessions would have to prove their case.

On the other aspect of the question, the issues were debated in the wrong order. In 1997 Heinz Schleusser, Finance Minister of North-Rhine-Westphalia, argued in vain that the scope for setting tax rates was governed by the extent to which subsidies were removed, not the other way round. And in the event it did indeed turn out to be the more complicated and ultimately unfeasible procedure – first to propose rates, then to haggle over how to finance them. Schleusser's proposal embodies the main principles of any reform programme: the tradition of governing via taxation policy must be abandoned.

As far as state subsidies are concerned, these must be given openly by direct grants. Any reform worthy of the name must include the removal of subventions as far as possible and a corresponding lowering of tax rates. This will lead to less tax being paid in all income groups – in so far as those concerned were not already in a position to make maximum use of the available opportunities for deductions and tax relief.

The moment of truth has arrived for our taxation policies. Can the power of the bureaucrats and lobby groups be broken, so that this burning topic can be opened up to public discussion? This is the challenge the SPD must grasp if it is to prove its ability to develop a coherent financial policy and identify the subjects that need to be addressed. Today, the SPD finds itself unexpectedly facing the task of modernizing not only Social Democrat philosophies but also those of the Liberals. The FDP as it is today seems to have lost interest in retaining and cultivating its historical values. It is therefore left to the SPD to summon the courage and strength to meet, through a package of modern, supportive and proactive policies, the demands being made on the Germans of today.

3

The Future of the Parties

Everywhere in Germany aficionados of the confrontational mentality appear set on blocking all frank and realistic discussion of positions that have become unsustainable. For decades many of the leading figures in all political parties have stubbornly defended their ideological position, come what may, and have talked themselves hoarse cajoling the caucus of their own supporters. Anxiously, timidly, the parties have tiptoed round subjects such as the reform of the public sector and provision for state employees, the need for increased flexibility in the labour market and the prize example of farm subsidies.

The nation is fed up with all this. The electoral victory of the SPD in 1998 brought fresh hopes and opened up exciting new possibilities. No less challenging is the opportunity to convert electoral success into increased support for the party itself. For a while after the election the new mood of optimism in the country gave the party carte blanche, a symbol of the nation's trust and an acceptance of the party's mandate to put its new programmes into practice. But this cannot be achieved without a fundamental modernization of all the parties, the SPD above all. I will therefore set out to identify where the structural problems lie, so that modernization of society can go hand in hand with modernization of the Social Democratic Party.

A glance at the situation in the rest of the world shows that the political systems in America, Japan and virtually all the developed countries confront similar problems. Nowhere is there a serious threat to democracy. But it is a central feature of the crisis in the development of informed political opinion that there has been a dramatic change in the nature of the relationship between the citizen and the state, as between the citizen and the political parties. It is a change manifested in the increasing lack of attention paid to the state and the parties, and in a growing sense of frustration.

The parties are no better off than the big corporations. They are closely linked to these corporations on all levels – committees, working parties and so on – yet at the end of the 1990s the question, banal in itself, as to what use the parties still serve, has receded into the background. The parties seem to be at the eye of the storm. What occupies their attention is their internal political struggles, as exemplified in 1997–8 first by the SPD's debate over the choice of their candidate for Chancellor, then by the discussions surrounding the leadership of the CDU and CSU. Every party has its problems with 'modernizers', but the more vital questions facing the party organizations were pushed into the background. At the same time it was apparent that the modernizers were all attempting, not with their parties but against them, to reform their political programmes and abandon entrenched ideological positions. This is the significance of the most striking slogan in the British Labour Party's campaign of 1997: 'New Labour – New Britain!' Modernize in order to govern, then govern in order to modernize.

The shortcomings revealed in the course of these efforts at modernization are as apparent in the SPD as in all the other parties, and the clearest symptom is the sense of fatigue that has settled over each organization. Membership of all parties declined in the 1980s and 1990s: the SPD, for instance, lost 11.5 per cent of its members in the western *Länder* between 1991 and 1995. The trend was halted in 1997 but still has to be reversed.

One of the most vital factors here is whether people have the confidence that answers to outstanding problems will in fact be forthcoming. The study commissioned by the oil giant Shell in 1997 is highly revealing in this respect. Confronted by their central fear, namely that of losing their jobs, the young people polled in this survey said they had lost confidence in the ability of any of the parties to deal with the problems facing the country.

But there are also other aspects of the situation. In his book *Children of Freedom* (1997), the sociologist Ulrich Beck wrote:

Young people are attracted to what politics leaves out. They hate
associations with their formal structures and their – as they see it
– crabbed and dishonest so-called 'unselfish' commitment to good
works. These young people vote with their feet, stay away. Even
the GDR authorities underestimated the explosive effect of this
attitude.

The typical Social Democrat is probably no longer in the full
flush of youth – just 7.4 per cent of the members are under the
age of 30. The membership of the Young Socialists has fallen by
more than half since the middle of the 1980s. University students
are in general reluctant to join established organizations to fight
for reforms. So the question becomes more and more urgent –
who is going to do the 'dirty work'? Where are new ideas to come
from, if the central political organizations and institutions in the
country are dominated by traditionally minded men and women
who have one eye on their careers? In the *Land* of Brandenburg
and the other East German *Länder* there are seats on local councils
which can hardly be filled because so few are willing to put their
names forward. A bitter phrase is going the rounds: 'Democracy
is losing its democrats.'

This lack of involvement by the younger generation is in danger
of turning into an outright crisis. For a long time membership of
the CDU and SPD had been getting older, but both had been
able to draw on the massive increase in membership during the
1970s. But if nothing radical happens, things will go rapidly downhill. Young members of the trade-union movement and other
organized support groups, traditional sources for the recruitment
of future party officials, simply rule themselves out. The 'generation contract', which preserved the tradition of party membership in the family and its social environment, has all but run its
course. The generation of 'What's in it for me?' may take part in
demonstrations and in collecting signatures for petitions, but the
political process with its agendas and its parliamentary debates
bores them stiff.

An internal investigation undertaken by the SPD in North-
Rhine-Westphalia in 1997 – a follow-up to *The SPD From Within*,
a study published in the mid-1980s of which I was co-editor –
revealed that the active core of the party, which did most of the
honorary work in the local constituencies, had remained stable. But
the number of activists ready to take part in election campaigns,

protest actions and the like has noticeably declined. At the beginning of the 1980s they made up 12 per cent; today it is only 6 per cent. The loyal party servant who began his career by posting placards and ended up, if he was lucky, as a member of his local council is a dying race.

However, this decline also has its positive side. In the old days there were 200-per-cent party members, men and women alike, who were not only convinced that they always had the right answers but also that they knew exactly where the source of the problems lay, and could describe in detail how the situation would develop after their party's victory. They not only had an unshakeable faith but also a missionary zeal. And if by chance they did not have a ready answer to a particular problem, then the only self-doubt they allowed themselves was a guilty feeling that they had not listened patiently enough to their political mentors, not studied their speeches and writings sufficiently closely.

Such attitudes are as remote today as the events in Jurassic Park, and such utterly committed party members have acquired almost dinosaur status. The person who says today, and really believes it, 'the party is always right', and who supports every resolution and every item of the party's programme, needs psychological treatment. Today's average party member would be rather a '70 per cent supporter', whose attitude would be 'my party is often right', or 'right most of the time'.

But the majority of people, over 90 per cent in fact, belong to no party. Their sober conclusion is that sometimes one party is right, sometimes another – on occasion the one more right than the other. Fifteen or twenty years ago it was sufficient to know that a man lived in a town of 100,000 inhabitants, was Catholic and a regular church-goer, in order to conclude with virtual certainty that he would vote CDU or CSU. On the other hand, a trade-unionist working in a large factory in an industrial conurbation would be expected to vote SPD. But today such things no longer count when it comes to predicting political preferences.

The parties are facing a great opportunity to turn these new, shifting patterns of political preference to their own advantage. Their existing structures, including that of the SPD, do not yet reflect the new spirit abroad in society, a spirit that is again coming to be identified with the SPD. The old image of the party, with its meetings in smoke-filled rooms and local halls, has not greatly changed, nor has the feeling of powerlessness on the part of many of its members. Their first experience of their local branch is often depressing. Many are looking for an opportunity to engage in political analysis and to work out solutions to pressing problems. They want to play their part in the formation of political opinion which the constitution lays down as one of the fundamental functions of political parties, as well as in the realization of their aims through the activities of parliament. They are looking for intellectual discussions rather than cosy branch meetings – an opportunity that all too rarely presents itself but which must be developed in order to meet people's desire to take part in the decision-making process through the agency of the parties. Investigations conducted among party members have repeatedly revealed a feeling of impotence and insignificance, a feeling of being excluded from forming party opinion.

Ulrich Pfeiffer criticized the SPD for having become a 'party of inflexible supporters with time on their hands' (there is, incidentally, a similar characterization of the CDU). The rigid system of a regionally organized hierarchy, which dominates the decision-making process, encourages regional inflexibility and takes up a great deal of time, says Pfeiffer, and anyone who wants to acquire even a modicum of influence on the conduct of affairs, 'has to spend a lot of time making himself known to the various working parties and committees. Without being on the spot and having time to spare, there is hardly any hope that one will be able to influence opinion. And it is also to be recommended, of course, that one does not move house.'

Those in positions of responsibility in economic life and representatives of occupations subject to strong competitive pressure are inevitably under-represented, while employers are scared off. In complex voting procedures in committees and other bodies, opinions are played off against each other until a position is reached where they can be reconciled with traditional views. This is the root of that structural conservatism which measures all new topics and problems against sacred dogma and party resolutions.

The debate in Germany on the future role of the parties is not new, nor has there been any shortage of realistic assessments of the situation. In 1977 Social Democrats in the Lower Rhine district put a controversial proposal to the annual party congress, pointing to the ideological controversy between the different wings of the party as the source of their problems. Virtually all the proposals for reform turned into debates between experts, incomprehensible to the members at large, conducted in a jargon that even long-serving ministers could not follow. This inability to consolidate basic ideas in a single package led to a loss of confidence in the government of Helmut Schmidt within the various factions in the party during the early phases of his administration, and the discrepancy between grand design and the rough-and-tumble of practical politics still haunts the SPD today. The party cannot but be damaged by this contradiction if the link between these two aspects is lost and one of them gains the upper hand.

One of the structural problems is how to allocate particular areas of activity among the ten internal working parties. In a scheme virtually impenetrable to outsiders, there are separate areas of competence for each of these bodies: the Working Party on Employment Problems, responsible for matters arising from worker participation; the Social Democratic Women's Group, which handles women's affairs and family matters; the Young Socialists, who continue to enjoy the results of the totally unjustified assumption that they are especially competent to handle matters involving juveniles and adolescents; the Association of Social Democratic lawyers; the Association of Social Democratic Health Workers; the Association of the Over-60s, and the rest.

The exclusivity and rigidity of this structure raises difficulties. There may be a lack of feedback, resulting in an excessively narrow concentration of attention on the activities of one working party or the other. Such cases cause new members of the party to see it as a kind of closed community into which they will only be received, and in which their contribution will only be appreciated, after they have worked their way up step by step.

I have deliberately exaggerated the shortcomings of the system, because the numbers of those who peremptorily reject all new ideas, using their influence in the media to impose their conception of what constitutes 'political correctness', are still considerable, particularly among those on the left. The rebels of 1968, many of them now approaching retirement age, invested a great deal in the formulation of their aims, putting their formulae and their symbolic slogans, together with the familiar perceptions of the day, into a succession of motions and demands. Programmes for action were drawn up and passed by majority vote. But they are not programmes for solving the problems of the present. Those on the left who yesterday were agitating for change often spend their time today defending the old *dirigiste* ideas embodied in the model of the redistributive welfare state. Deep down, many party functionaries are still wedded to the principle that only the intervention of the state can establish the benign balance between the individual and society – never the market.

The paralysis that has gripped organizational life in many areas has prevented the parties from facing both the philosophical and the practical realities of the situation. We must accept the fact that politics, especially for young people, has become a peripheral concern. We can readily arouse interest in specific issues but much less readily, if at all, in institutionalized politics. Perhaps the solution might lie in the establishment of 'concept groups' alongside local branches, in which, with the help of the new media, fresh concepts could be freely and flexibly discussed. In a number of towns in North-Rhine-Westphalia so-called 'Contact Groups of Progressive Social Democratic Women' have been formed, cutting across the party's traditional fields of competence and with no formal statutes, to discuss subjects such as town planning, traffic and the environment, economic policy and social matters. The popularity of such groups shows that there is a growing need for involvement in freely accessible political activity.

We must take the organizational problems of the parties seriously, because only to the superficial gaze are they internal problems. The public is aware of what is happening. During the Kohl era confidence in politicians and parties, according to the findings of a poll by the Emnid organization, fell from around 50 to 20 per cent. And in a league table measuring the respect and popularity enjoyed by all occupational groups in society, politicians occupied 25th place!

A general suspicion has arisen that politicians are basically a clique of opportunist self-seekers looking for patronage and a means of exercising power. There was a sharp rise between the early 1980s and the 1990s in those who were of the opinion that 'there was a great number of dishonest people among those politicians who govern the country'. This antipathy is now spreading to include public administration, long a source of admiration. The debate on the financing of the parties and their delegates is not that interesting in itself, but it has considerable symbolic importance as an indication of how far the public debate on our democratic institutions has deteriorated.

For myself I cannot conceive how the urgent challenges of the future can possibly be met without political parties. Popular demonstrations and single-issue movements have their attractions, but in the last analysis they do not mesh with the workings of the parliamentary system. The experience of the Greens shows that it is not sufficient to set up an informal ad hoc structure and expect it to function as the parliamentary arm of lobbyists and protesters. Every parliamentary decision, like every inevitable compromise, leaves tensions and disappointments on both sides. Any attempt to apply the procedures of compromise and consensus-building to the activities of the one-issue movement is doomed to failure.

The task facing the parties is to reclaim for themselves the great issues that confront the world. It will not be easy. Political observers in other Western countries point to the radical shift in values and the rapid changes in the media landscape. Some commentators in Japan and America are talking of a 'videocracy' – it would no longer be the political parties and the public who decided the issues for discussion but the mass media.

Politics is becoming increasingly personalized and emotionalized. At the same time it is only one subject of interest among many, from sport to domestic problems. And those who do concern themselves with politics are more interested in the attitudes of leading politicians than in the political programme of a particular party. The parties' internal means of communication, and especially their organs, have lost their relevance in the general flood of information and comment. The line followed by a particular daily newspaper is becoming less and less the expression of a particular *Weltanschauung*. The days of the mass inculcation of a party political line have gone, probably for ever. No longer can the expectation prevail that a party will consistently convey a coherent view of the world, or that a paper will faithfully publish the party's attitude to this, that and the other. Nor is there any cause to regret this.

It is also becoming increasingly difficult for the political parties to cope with the numerous committees, working parties, etc. that have sprung up to create crossover possibilities between the federal government, provincial governments and local authorities. They are at sixes and sevens. In one *Land* a party may strongly oppose procedures of which their colleagues in another *Land* equally strongly approve. The political integration at national, regional and local authority level makes for inner disintegration of the parties, since political survival on one level may entail dissociation at another level. For example, in the Bundestag the SPD initially opposed increasing the rate of value-added tax, whereas in the parliaments of the *Länder* it approved the increase as essential to their budgets. It is a trap in which all the parties can be, and have been, caught at one time or another.

All these investigations into the state of the parties are as complex as the developments in society itself. But they have a common core. People are no longer interested in retaining the old, rusty machinery of a state in which each citizen's main concern is to feather his own nest. It is a paradoxical situation. The accumulated backlog of proposed reforms makes the need for new policies ever more urgent, and the parties and related institutions are the only forces that can deal with this backlog – both the cause of the malaise and the hope for its cure. Countess Marion Dönhoff struck the nail on the head when she wrote in her book *Civilise Capitalism* (1997) that all the talk about people being weary of politics was superficial; when one looked more closely, one found that they were in fact expressing the wish that, far from becoming less active, politicians would act more determinedly and responsibly.

The parties have not come to the end of the road. But they are too far behind the times, too slow to adapt. They must quickly return to being the centres of social discourse, the starting-points in the search for solutions. Encouraging signs were already visible in the elections of 1994, which showed that the turn-out had stopped falling and the main parties had consolidated their positions, in spite of an increased incidence of split votes not only between first and second preferences but also between the elections for local authorities, provincial parliaments and the federal parliament.

As far as the Social Democrats are concerned, these positive trends were confirmed by the elections in Lower Saxony in 1998. Yet the warning uttered in 1995 by the political analyst Ulrich von Alemann is still valid: 'The parties of the future will have to redouble their efforts to regain their respect and their authority, otherwise they will rapidly slither into the next crisis.' At the top of Alemann's list of twenty proposals for a reform of party political democracy in Germany is reform of the organization of the parties themselves – a reform that must not be allowed to stop at constitutional matters or the party political system itself.

The conclusion reached in all studies into the extremist parties of the far right in European politics is that a polarization can be prevented if the centre parties can put forward a new and convincing social programme. It is the obligation of all parties to strive to remove the blockages in the political system. The key to gaining the confidence of the electorate is the manifest ability to solve problems. Political choices are governed by the concrete job experiences of the electors and in economic matters, as well as by the circumstances of family life and enjoyment of leisure time. Electors therefore prefer pragmatic proposals to comprehensive intellectual programmes.

The problem of traffic jams, for instance, which cost a great deal both in economic and ecological terms and put a strain on everybody's nerves, is capable of being successfully solved. But people react with scepticism when politicians put it on their agenda, for they have come to expect that politicians will avoid such concrete problems as far as possible. Success will come to the person who manages to combine a sense of vision with radical, pragmatic proposals and to put tangible improvements in train. That, at least, is what New Labour and the American Democrats have discovered.

It sounds a mere matter of course, but the SPD would be taking a great step forwards if in future it stopped to reflect, before passing any resolution, whether, and how, it could gain majority support for that resolution in the country as a whole. This is a precondition for the relevance of any resolution. The problem is that the parties are everywhere too concerned with themselves. The question of whether one could get a majority for this or that proposal is branded as populist or opportunist. Such an attitude is quite alien to my way of looking at things. How, after all, can an organization's self-esteem be based on the judgement of a minority? For all democrats it is a matter of course that they take their lead from the concerns of the majority to whom they look in order to be elected.

Tony Blair and New Labour: Pragmatism with Vision

The election of New Labour in the UK in 1997 shows that there is a way of escaping from the depressing apathy towards politics and politicians that prevails in Germany. New Labour is distinguished by its combination of pragmatism and vision, and marks the arrival of a new political culture, a change of direction which leads beyond the old party political structures and rituals but which is as yet showing itself only hesitantly and sporadically in the policies of the SPD.

There is life after the dinosaurs. Today New Labour is the fastest-growing party in the world. The average age of its members is 43, and almost half the new members are women. In the general election of 1 May 1997 the party won over a large section of the middle class for the first time – 60 per cent of the new members belong to this group. Never before had a Labour leader enjoyed such a parliamentary majority. It enabled him to discipline dissidents within his own ranks and to avoid internal conflicts over his political course by reminding his colleagues of the power of the party members to 'vote with their feet'.

Blair's often reiterated principle is to stop looking back and seeking to clear up the detritus of the past but instead to look forward with vision and imagination. The time of dogma and ideology is past. Blair has modernized in order to govern; at the same time, he was elected to govern in order to be able to modernize. He found himself in a position to set the most ossified, most backward-looking left-wing party in Europe on a moderniz- ing course, while introducing discipline into the party ranks. 'New Labour – New Britain.'

Blair's triumphant occupation of No. 10 Downing Street caused political commentators serious problems of interpretation. Was the new government, in economic and socio-political terms, to the right of the CDU, as the *Frankfurter Allgemeine Zeitung* main- tained, or was it experiencing the change to a popular party that the SPD went through when it adopted its so-called 'Godesberg Programme' in 1959? What role would Blair play if there were a swing in Europe as a whole towards social democratic par- ties? Labour's new pragmatism no longer fits into the traditional categories of left and right. There is a comparison to be made in purely party terms with the SPD at the time of the Godesberg Programme, but in fact the development goes far beyond that.

Tony Blair was a party rebel but he did not stand alone. A start had already been made on dismantling ideological structures and jettisoning yesterday's answers to today's problems after the catastrophic defeat in the election of 1983. Blair had just entered the House of Commons. Defeated in the election of 1979, riven with internal divisions throughout the early 1980s and written off as a serious political force, Labour fought its way back under the leadership, successively, of Neil Kinnock, John Smith and Tony Blair. Reforms within the party itself opened a channel to the political middle ground and thus to a return to government. New Labour stands, above all, for a break with the traditional structure of the Labour Party, i.e. the alliance between party, trade unions and attached organizations. Blair has made no concessions to the unions, which might have expected that there would be a return to the old days. Since the time of Margaret Thatcher their influence has continued to be marginal.

The decisive step in the internal reform of the Labour Party was taken at the party conference in Brighton in 1993. Here it was decided that parliamentary candidates would in future be selected not by the individual unions and members of the local constituencies but only by constituency members themselves. The principle was now 'One member, one vote', a principle that amounted to a structural revolt against entrenched traditional interests. In the past the unions, through their block vote, had commanded 40 per cent of delegates' votes, leaving the remaining 60 per cent for constituency members and members of parliament.

A further change came the following year with the amendment of the famous Clause 4 of the party constitution – the age-old commitment to the nationalization of the means of manufacture, distribution and exchange. In place of this came a bland statement of commitment to the principles of democratic socialism. This change was so radical because Clause 4 had always been regarded as a sacred cow by the traditional Labour Party. The move made it clear to the public that the party had a will for change and a preparedness to abandon out-of-date principles that had hitherto always been regarded as unassailable.

Taken by themselves, these reforms have scant relevance to the needs of the German SPD. But their effect, political significance and social impact are comparable to the SPD's experience since the provincial elections in Lower Saxony in March 1998 and the election of Gerhard Schröder as the party's candidate for the chancellorship. The days are over when what was practicable was considered not social democratic, and what was social democratic was not practicable.

But there is a comparison to be made between the two parties' basic tenets. 'We have reformed our party,' said Tony Blair in the course of the 1997 election campaign, 'and that proves that we can govern the country.' The internal reform of the 'old' Labour Party was what triggered Blair's success. Compared with the state of affairs in the 1980s, Labour achieved a quite remarkable success, stimulated by a sustained campaign to make it respond to the winds of change. This is an achievement not to be underestimated – and it is a test still facing parts of our own SPD.

The rise of Tony Blair would be unthinkable without Kinnock and Smith. Similarly, Labour's victory in 1997 would be unthinkable without Blair. Something had been missing up to that point. It took a long while for modernization to show itself in the form of electoral victories. What had been missing was the charisma, the sense of mission, of plausibility and dependability, that this man embodied – a union of party, programme and personality. And it was, above all, the British middle classes, politically confident under Mrs Thatcher but socially and economically uncertain of themselves, that came to accept first Tony Blair and his modernization programme, then New Labour itself, with its realistic, forward-looking manifesto. Blair took the broad spectrum of new ideas in his party and converted them into concrete, realistic, viable projects. This was what the country wanted. Blair called it 'Operation Victory'.

According to analyses made by BBC commentators, it was, in particular, enterprising young people, above all women, from the ambitious middle classes who had up to then tended to be non-voters, who responded to this programme of modernization. They voted for a man who wore neither hob-nailed boots on his feet nor a bowler hat on his head. It was 'the American style' – outwardly frank and sympathetic, inwardly tough.

Many are cautious about the Blair government. It is not difficult, they say, to adopt successful policies if one comes into office at a moment when the country is enjoying an economic boom. There is some truth in this. Anybody who is elected at such a moment finds it easier to pursue his policies and finance his programmes than someone who finds himself saddled with the task of first clearing up the mess left by his predecessor.

Another criticism one hears is that in fact the Blair government is doing nothing other than carry on the deregulation and privatization policies of the Tories – the same old policies dressed up in new clothes. The Prime Minister is also criticized for conducting the affairs of the country through the media: videos are shown at the beginning of every political meeting, with pretty pictures and slogans taking the place of discussions of real substance. Part of the same picture – unique in Europe, and in the opinion of both British and German commentators indicative of how things will be in the future – is the way the election campaign was fought almost exclusively in the media. More flexible forms of political communication are becoming standard practice, with thoughts and ideas conveyed through public channels instead of in private committee meetings.

But what do things look like after two years of the Blair government? Is the new regime one of attractive visions and mere slogans, like 'Cool Britannia', or is it really achieving what it promised in its election manifesto?

At this point I should like to make a digression on the subject of the personalization of politics and the ways it is being used in appeals to the electorate.

On the strength of his personal background alone – born into a Tory household, a barrister by training, influenced by Christian socialist modes of thought – Tony Blair was predestined to be a protagonist of consensus politics. Labour allowed him to introduce discipline into their ranks because they realized that without it they would stand no chance with the voters. Left-wing political commentators have sometimes charged him with an authoritarian tendency. In an interview on NBC, for instance, it was suggested that Britain was on the way to becoming a one-party state in which the various political alternatives were indistinguishable.

Behind these accusations lurks a far more serious problem that Germany also has, namely the challenging by pragmatic modernizers, in all sectors and institutions of society, of a status quo whose justification has become only ideological. The situation at the end of the 1990s recalls the moment when the sociologist Max Weber saw the time coming in democratic parliamentary systems when a charismatic leader would emerge – a moment when a desperate situation can only be rescued by a man who clears the decks and starts anew. Weber described the mechanisms of bureaucratic control as well as the conditions in which over-bureaucratized institutions are compelled to submit to a new mediator – given that things have reached an impasse and the formal and procedural legitimacy of state institutions and interest groups is declining so rapidly that their very existence is called in question.

Have we not reached the point today when the political parties must allow themselves to be asked this very question? We have repeatedly seen that charisma can be of overriding importance in an election campaign – indeed, success in an election may depend on it, and consequently also the legitimization of all those involved in it. If this is the case, the charismatic leader must be permitted to circumvent established practices and interests, to put forward new projects that go beyond existing frameworks, and to replace a dour adherence to precedent with fascinating new visions. The charismatic moment is an integral factor in the democratic process because it uncovers and profiles political options which have been reduced to the lowest common denominator and virtually dropped out of sight as far as the average elector is concerned.

An excessive or one-sided personalization of political issues does, of course, face the danger that the power of the media in the dissemination and interpretation of these issues may reach unacceptable proportions. At the same time a certain degree of personalization corresponds to our everyday experience and is sensible. I have never met a politician who, in the course of a private meeting behind closed doors, pulled the party rule-book out of his pocket and proceeded to check what it said, or to bring to bear on a current problem decisions that were made some time in the past. It is fully justifiable to enquire after an individual's fundamental attitudes if one wants to gain a feeling of how he will decide when the time comes.

A comparison of people's concrete, pragmatic decisions with their behaviour in discussions of the party programme would cause many to rub their eyes in astonishment. For that reason alone the desire to know more about the personality of our heroes is far more productive than the question of the basic principles that may have been agreed upon as the result of an anonymous vote taken at some meeting. But there is also an internal party process, dependent on personalities with fixed spheres of influence who establish the degree of social control necessary to prevent political and social obligations from being played down, or even ignored. All this gives grounds enough for one to plead for the renovation of the party to which one belongs, to which one owes one's loyalty and which one wishes success.

In the UK the demands of everyday politics show that the problems with which Labour has to deal are the problems with which all parties have to deal. The opposition of interest groups and the laborious efforts to mediate between different points of view; the difficulties involved in devising transparent and comprehensible means of formulating complex demands – such problems cannot be solved by political showmanship.

But in its first year in office Labour also showed its ability to take tough decisions. Taking over and extending the policies of the Conservatives causes internal problems for New Labour. Up till now the party organization has been able to handle these tensions very efficiently. Labour's courage in facing up to controversial issues should give the German Social Democrats confidence. After their victory in 1998 the SPD has been called upon to make structural changes in the party which must inevitably lead to controversy, both within the party itself and in the public at large. Labour managed to escape this controversy to a large extent because the severest cuts had already been made by the Conservatives. But the vital point is that Blair and New Labour have linked their necessary reform measures and their policy of restraint to a guarantee of new safeguards. This is the source of the confidence that the British government enjoys today, a government that has succeeded in fulfilling many of its promises.

In the UK, as everywhere else, the rises and falls in the government's stock depend on the success of its policies. Labour's list of successes incorporates radical programmes for reform for which the British electorate has given it a clear mandate.

An observation in passing. Too often Labour's success is measured in Germany by reference to those items on the political agenda which are of special importance to us, whereas paramount to the British are such questions as the reform of the constitution. Devolution, for example, the decentralization of power and the transfer of sovereign powers from Westminster to Scotland and Wales, was set in train, as were the introduction of proportional representation in elections for the European and Scottish parliaments and the establishment of the post of mayor for London. Then there is the £3.5 million 'Welfare to Work' programme, financed by the 'windfall tax' on the profits made by privatized companies, which aims to offer jobs to 250,000 young men and women under the age of 25 and thus take them out of the welfare system. The key concept is not lifelong employment but lifelong employability.

Take also the question of education. The British government has pumped £2.5 million into what is to German eyes a remarkably decrepit school system. But at the same time new standards were introduced into school education, with strict measures for enforcing those standards. All 4-year-olds are to be guaranteed a place in a nursery school, and in primary schools there are to be extra periods devoted to reading and mathematics. Every school is to receive £1,000 for new books.

In the last analysis, what forced Labour into action were the alarming shortcomings in the welfare system. The public saw that politicians recognized the problems that confronted them, the public, every day. By abolishing all taboos, Blair made himself a rebel. It is we who set the agenda, he said, and the challenge is to solve the problems that face us. He rallied the party behind him with programmes linked to the problems of the people and of the business community, programmes that had been widely discussed in the party but only with reservations – education, the balance between employment and the needs of the economy, the fight against crime, a new social contract.

The strength of the Blair government can also be seen in the way differing opinions, and even minor revolts within Labour's own ranks, can be controlled and confined. Anyone who follows the course of politics in the UK can clearly see that New Labour is no mere electoral organization. Open debates take place as always, but linked with the determination not to see power taken away from it after a single term in office, as has been the fate of every Labour government up till now. New Labour is already a considerable way down the path of the 'Third Way'. As a term, the 'Third Way' signifies a departure both from the economic individualism of the Thatcher era, which equated competition with confrontation, and from the demand to be allowed to make unrestricted claims on the welfare state. Instead of redistributive policies the Labour party evolved a supply-side socialism which emphasizes the individual's obligations both to himself and to society, incorporating the ideal of equality of opportunity. 'To govern for the many, not the few' – such was its promise. And it will be judged by how it lives up to this promise.

A man who does a job of work must be allowed to keep the lion's share of the money he earns. Blair's business manifesto guarantees more flexible competitive markets, better qualified workers, investment guarantees and help for the middle classes. In return, employers will underwrite the government's agreement to the European Social Chapter, accept a minimum wage and make various other concessions. The unions are prepared to accept that there will be no return to a regulated labour market.

In June 1996, when Blair stood on the threshold of coming to power, there appeared in the journal *Wirtschaftswoche* an article entitled 'Must Left-Wingers be Socialists?' Blair has answered this question in his own way, for example through New Labour's taxation policy, which is not slanted towards penalizing employers but at promoting the efficiency of the system. 'A person who is financially successful', said Blair, 'has our blessing' – adding that the British left wing had been founded on the principle of setting out to cure poverty. The SPD would do well to remember such things as it embarks on its own programme of reforms.

4

The Beginnings of a
New Corporatism

1996 and 1997 marked the end of consensus and co-operation. Key moments were the collapse of the Alliance for Employment and the crucial debate that went on from 1995 to 1997. This meant that one of the central structural principles of the social market economy was abandoned. So-called Rhineland capitalism, the model of an institutionalized compromise between the interests of the state, employers and employees, came to be regarded as a fudge which was putting the brake on innovation and progress.

It is alarming to see how far we have moved away from a positive, constructive view of corporate management. At an international trade fair in Munich in the spring of 1998, for example, leading business associations put their weight behind the campaign to re-elect Helmut Kohl and announced the creation of half a million new jobs in the course of the year. The very next day they were forced to backtrack on their offer. First they cut back the figure to 350,000, then to 100,000 – if we were lucky. It was a slap in the face not only for the government, which would have done better to reject such help, but also for the employers, for whom it was a public relations disaster.

A new style of politics is emerging, with more open forms of discussion and co-operation. But this new mood of compromise is evidently unwelcome, first and foremost to employers' organizations, whose muscle-flexing cannot disguise the fact that their influence is in decline. New companies in the service industries rarely join these organizations. In East Germany barely a third of firms belong to them, and their power to call individual firms to heel when particular policies are at issue is growing less and less.

Gerhard Schröder, on the other hand, openly advocates a kind of 'staged corporatism', in which politicians sit down with the most progressive and innovatory employers, unions and works committees to get to grips with a concrete problem. The faint-hearted are not invited, nor, necessarily, are official representatives on every occasion. Leading functionaries on both employers' and employees' sides find it difficult to come to terms with such manifestations of a proactive state. Fear of a pragmatic consensus makes them restless. They are so firmly stuck in the quagmire of tradition and conventional practices that they can see no future in such innovations. Yet it is precisely this pragmatic consensus that is the nub of the social market economy.

From the very beginning the German Confederation of Industries (BDI) had its problems with the concept of the social market economy. When in the 1950s Economics Minister Ludwig Erhard pleaded for a competitive economy in which cartels were largely banned, the BDI rose up in arms against what it called 'a system alien to the German economy' and 'the patronizing attitude of a bureaucratic state'. Such an accusation levelled at the father of the social market economy sounds ridiculous today. But when one compares Erhard's conception of the state with that of the industrialists of that time, one can see what is at stake. Erhard wanted a strong state with firmly delineated functions: within this framework economic forces would be able to develop freely. The BDI, on the other hand, openly attacked what it saw both as the 'unbridled liberalism' and the 'authoritarianism' of such a philosophy. A strong state as conceived by Erhard could not but be seen by the BDI as a threat because it retained control of the system and would not allow itself to be exploited but guaranteed open competition, productivity and transparency, whereas established interests wanted to divide up the state and the economy among themselves. Erhard's was not a state in which secret deals could be made behind closed doors. At the climax of the struggle over the Anti-Cartel Act in 1954, after the BDI had watered down the proposals in one attack after another, Erhard dug in his heels. The constitution, he said in the Bundestag on 24 March, was being directly challenged by sectional interests: 'If every group seeks special protection for itself, people will lose more and more of their freedom, more and more of their sense of security.'

Is it possible for us to revive this awareness of the need for a proactive state which reconciles conflicting interests? In 1954 pragmatists and businessmen with a sense of social responsibility succeeded in rescuing a consensus. Men like Winkhaus from Mannesmann, Henle from Klöckner and Ziervogel from Ruhrgas signed an open letter that forced the BDI to co-operate. In the same spirit, in March 1998 a similar group of pragmatically minded employers criticized their leaders over their attitude in the argument over sick pay. Hans-Olaf Henkel, president of the BDI, sought to mediate and was promptly attacked by the CSU as a man 'unfit to negotiate over political issues because he lacked a firm sense of political direction'. According to Hans Michelbach of the CSU, such attitudes had negative repercussions for the economy. Such views are an expression of the panic felt by cliques and special-interest groups which attach no value to consensus but which at the same time realize that their days are numbered.

The preparedness to seek pragmatic consensus is the precondition for concerted action to tackle the urgent problems that confront us. However, the conditions for a successful corporatist resolution of our problems and for a new co-operative economic policy have changed dramatically since the 1960s. At that time there was virtually full employment; today, we have mass unemployment. Then, the German Federal Republic registered a rapid growth in gross domestic product, with scope for redistribution of the increase; today, in contrast, we face growth without employment, coupled with a steep rise in the taxes and deductions that affect all private households, while real earnings are even falling slightly, resulting in a decline in consumer demand.

The state of the German corporatist economy in the final phase of the Kohl administration was depressing. Norbert Walter, head of research at Deutsche Bank, published an article in the journal *Capital* in January 1997, in which he summed up the inward-looking, self-centred, decaying German capitalist system:

The social market economy, the trademark of post-war Germany, was an export model, and at the end was exported in its entirety. We have come to the end of the road as corporatists, surrounded by large, noisy groups sitting round large tables, looking for points of reference, incapable of arguing our case, reluctant to make decisions, afraid to strike out in new directions.

An image to reflect the dilemma of traditional German corporatist culture that needs to preserve its principles, while at the same time trying to develop new ways of balancing conflicting interests, would be what one might call a 'quicksand society'. A man who falls into quicksand sinks more rapidly the more he struggles and tries to get out. Only by reacting in an unexpected and unusual way, making measured, deliberate swimming movements, can he save himself. Moreover, not only will the man who thrashes about with his arms and legs go under, so also will the man who tries to go back.

What is happening at the moment seems to be that a handful of innovators – particularly, on the workers' side, from the works committees – are swimming their way out of the quicksand which is produced when the soil of entrenched ideologies and institutionalized procedures becomes increasingly churned up by social change and intensified competition. Others then make the situation worse by struggling to fight their way out, or try to rescue themselves with the help of yesterday's slogans and methods, instead of looking for new, pragmatic solutions. The culture of corporate bodies, at federal level, with its traditional cliques, its undisguisedly partisan attitudes and its ritualistic procedures, has ever less relevance and constructive influence. Urgent problems such as youth unemployment lie obviously beyond the reach of such bodies.

Similarly, the traditional wage-bargaining model is unable to stabilize these inherited forms because it is itself under pressure to change. Authoritative observers of the German system of industrial relations see a crisis looming, provoked above all by the situation in the employers' organizations. As Wolfgang Streeck predicted in an article written in February 1996:

> In the short term, the survival of local and regional wage agreements as a corrective to the labour market depends on the stability and commitment of employers' organizations. Continued unemployment will lead to further withdrawals from such organizations and from established wage agreements, with or without the tacit consent of local employees' representatives. Without strong representative employers' organizations there can be no local wage deals and in the long run probably no industrial trade unions either. This means that the unions are again facing the paradoxical situation they have faced in the past, namely that it is in their own interests to help reorganize the capitalist system.

Since the middle of the 1960s there has been a steep decline in the membership of employers' organizations, in some cases by as much as 70 per cent, reducing membership to a little over 40 per cent. It has not been an even development over this period but has rapidly accelerated since the mid-1980s. New companies in regional industries such as metalworking and electronics no longer bother to join.

Even more striking is the decline in membership on the part of employees. In eastern Germany – the former GDR – only a little over half of all employees worked in enterprises which belonged to an employers' association in 1994. In 1997 Norbert Blüm, then Minister of Labour, remarked bitterly that if association presidents were to spend a mere 10 per cent of their time on taking care of their members' interests, it would be a big step forward.

But the trade unions also have difficulty in retaining members. The number of workers in unions under the aegis of the German Trade Union Congress (DGB) fell between 1994 and 1995 by 4.2 per cent in the country as a whole – in eastern Germany the figure was 8.8 per cent, in the west 2.6 per cent. At first sight these figures do not appear particularly alarming, but between 1990 and 1995 the loss of members amounted to 10 per cent, and the trend continues. Average membership remains around 30 per cent.

The trade unions recognize the need for a modernization of the system of local wage negotiations. This is a vital matter for worker participation, for the number of employees represented neither on the board of directors nor in works councils has risen between the mid-1980s and the mid-1990s from 50.6 to 60.5 per cent. The significance of this dramatic development becomes even clearer when one realizes that at the end of the 1980s, in the old West Germany as it was, wages and working conditions were regulated over virtually the whole country by fixed agreements. This situation, exceptional in comparison with that in all other industrialized countries, now no longer exists. The 'German Model', with its integrated system of industrial relations, is facing its moment of truth – indeed, its day may even be past, without there being any other cogent model to take its place. In corporatism as in federalism it is not just a question of producing a system that will modify the effects of the contradictions in the present set-up – it is a question of creating a system that will produce pragmatic solutions to specific problems.

There are already signs of the emergence of a new corporate culture, with the outlines of a new alliance, to be detected in a new flexibility in negotiations over new regional wage settlements. Negotiated agreements on part-time working for older workers have shown that old ideological positions have, fortunately, been given up and that the parties are well on the way to establishing a basic consensus. In many cases it is the employees' representatives who are setting the pace. Experienced works councils are no longer prepared to continue in the old confrontational way because they see what harm a spirit of competitiveness can do, and because they know that only companies that can meet the demands of the market will be able to survive. They can also see that the growing burden of tax and social security deductions makes this impossible. In a joint article published in 1996 Wolfgang Streeck and Walter Riester recommended that the SPD and the unions should be prepared to emphasize the individual's responsibility for his own social security and for the funding of the welfare scheme as a whole. Everyone must be willing to shift his position.

In the eyes of many negotiators and commentators, the diagnosis that the traditional corporatist culture will change, added to the collapse of the Alliance for Employment in 1996, reduces the opportunities for a new alliance of the kind proposed by Gerhard Schröder. This overlooks, however, the fact that all neighbouring European countries which have been successful on the labour market in recent years have based their policies on the institution of a permanent dialogue between the negotiating partners and the state, in which practical issues are discussed. Tripartite alliances between the government, the employers and the trade unions to deal with matters such as unemployment and the reform of the welfare state already exist in a number of European countries. In Germany, however, in spite of its long tradition of social welfare legislation, no such alliance has yet been concluded. But with the new conditions in international markets, European integration and the pressure it exerts to modernize and consolidate, together with the restrictions placed on monetary and fiscal activity, the only alternative to consensus is stagnation.

Employment alliances in European countries derive as a rule from government initiatives. Unless the search for consensus on a new economic and welfare policy for Germany is made the central issue, it will lead nowhere. The autonomy of the negotiating parties and the political responsibilities of the government are not mutually exclusive. The government's task is to remind the parties of their responsibilities and make it clear that, if need arose, it would bring legislation to bear on its own account.

The most familiar example is the Netherlands, where the then Prime Minister Ruud Lubbers threatened that, in the event of no agreement being reached, the government would intervene and set a wage rate. The Wassenaar Agreement of 1982 lays down the framework for the reform of the nation's economy. It consists only of a few paragraphs. Consensus is arrived at not in every single point but in the form of joint presentations of the problems and an objective analysis. Such an alliance for economic growth and employment, as I would prefer to call it, could not, of course, put forward guidelines for determining wage rates or draw up official agreements on increases in employment. An agreed assessment of the situation and the scope for action must first be settled at national level; this would then lead to a series of decentralized alliances in individual regions and industries. This presupposes, however, central agreement on aims and procedures.

Unlike Germany, the Netherlands has established institutions where not only government, employers and workers but also outside independent experts regularly meet – and not only at moments of crisis. One such body, set up by umbrella organizations representing both employers and unions, regularly meets to discuss the mid- and long-term prospects for labour relations and adjust wage rates, in company with the socio-economic advisory board, whose proposals on matters of employment and economic policy, as well as on planned legislation, have in recent years almost become binding on all parties. After almost abolishing such institutions at the end of the 1970s, the Dutch revived them in order to deal with the crisis at the beginning of the 1980s.

A comparable scheme for Germany would need to involve similar forms of 'institutionalized confidence'. Such co-operative initiatives require a great deal of staying-power, as the above-mentioned case of the education and training programme for North-Rhine-Westphalia shows. There are four main topics which need to be addressed:

1. The framing of a wages policy geared to the needs of employment.

2. The lowering of wage added costs, combined with a reform of the taxation system.
3. The modernization of the welfare state and bringing the social security system into line with new forms of employment, such as those in the service sector, possibly by introducing agreed provisions for a 'joint wage', while at the same time extending the opportunities for workers to share in wealth-creation schemes.
4. Differentiated reductions in working hours which take account both of the employers' need for flexible working arrangements and the wishes of the workers.

As we succeed in integrating these topics into the agenda of our co-operative economic policy, so we shall discover that the more comprehensive the package, the easier the integration of the various interests. The question of employment policy, for instance, will inevitably touch on fundamental matters of education and qualification, and involve entirely new forms of advanced training. 'We need to set our sights on the facts and on what is pragmatically possible', said Wolfgang Streeck in an interview for the journal *Mitbestimmung* in June 1998. 'We need a combination of realism and consensus, instead of non-committal statements in press releases and meetings where each man speaks only for himself. The parties must be free to talk to each other openly and without preconceptions about the realities with which we all have to come to terms.'

When it comes to the matter of decentralization, attention will focus on the numerous agreements that have been reached at factory level, and thence on the role of worker participation. Since 1996, when the first such agreements on guaranteed employment were put on the public agenda, they have had a polarizing effect on the debate. Irritation has resulted from an absence of agreed definitions. While some see such agreements as offering a model strategy of flexibility, others are only prepared to call on them in moments of crisis. Because there is no unanimity about their aims, extreme positions become possible, right down to the demand by Hans-Olaf Henkel in 1998 that their scope should be extended to the utmost limit – a demand bound to be seen by the public as an open challenge to break existing wage agreements. Only today are the future of the national wage agreement system and the role of works agreements beginning to be soberly debated.

The system of worker participation is a German success story. It has become a basic element in the country's industrial life, a flexible strategy capable of adapting itself to new competitive conditions. The 35-member committee of experts from management, the unions and the outside world, which, on behalf of the Bertelsmann Foundation and the unions' Hans Böckler Foundation, examined the practice and the effects of worker participation over a period of two years, came to the conclusion that this participation was an advantage for industrial relations in Germany because in many companies it assisted the process of structural change and was thus a force for stability. The committee praised in particular the introduction of works agreements pledged to the retention of the existing workforce and the creation of new jobs.

At the time of one of the largest amalgamations of recent years – the international merger of Mercedes-Benz and Chrysler – the German worker participation model was taken over as part of the deal, and its advantages were a decisive argument in favour of making Germany the firm's headquarters. So impressed by the system of worker participation was he, that Jürgen Schrempp, Managing Director of Daimler-Benz, recommended to his American partners that they put it into place in their own factories – which they did.

Is worker participation therefore a model beyond discussion, a prototype of corporate industrial management and industrial relations? Beyond doubt it has the potential to become an instrument of industrial innovation, encouraging, as it does, the adoption of a path of 'co-operative modernization'. This has always been the path that Germany has followed when management and workers have found themselves forced to adapt to difficult economic conditions. It is a tradition that can be called upon when it is necessary to counter the risks inherent in future market developments. One might even say: 'It is not a case of which way the wind is blowing but of how we set our sails.'

This applies equally to guaranteeing the safety of existing jobs and creating new ones. Local agreements can make an important contribution to employment policies, provided they have support from the centre, i.e. from their national wage negotiators. If, for example, a firm is prepared to negotiate over medium-term investment plans, and the employees' side is willing to give certain complementary undertakings, this could prove a useful addition to the areas of worker participation. The crucial point is how the national wage-bargaining system can be combined with co-operation at works level.

There can still be a future for regional wage deals. But it is becoming less and less possible to impose them on management and workers. The weakening influence of employers' organizations is particularly worrying in this respect, for unless these organizations are strong, there can be no regional agreements. If there is to be a future for such agreements, they must take account of the growing need for flexibility. So too must the highly productive service industries, growth areas of the future, which make their own demands for flexibility. As a matter of principle both sides of industry have good reason to hold on to the system of local agreements. In spite of their sometimes extravagant rhetoric on the subject of deregulation, they too have a vested interest in retaining the basic elements of the labour market. If this interest appears in many cases to be on the wane at the present time, it could well be revived by a thorough reform of the entire system of negotiations and agreements.

Over recent years the German pattern of industrial relations has developed a number of different methods of adapting regional agreements to diverse sets of conditions, ranging from joint declarations and mutual assurances by the negotiating parties to proposals for alternative regulations and hardship provisions. Flexibility has progressed further in practice than in theory, yet is seldom adduced as an argument against an apparently deep-rooted opposition to modernization, precisely because there are no shared interpretations or agreed objectives.

For the organization and working practices of both the unions and the employers' associations a change of this kind would represent a considerable challenge. The organizational structures of both sides would have to reflect different priorities, assisted by what well-disposed critics have described as 'linesmen' – specialists charged with the task of immediately identifying departures from established resolutions and explaining to their superiors why they cannot agree to this or that proposal. The narrow-mindedness of many hardliners and idealists at all levels in their respective bureaucracies must not be allowed to hinder the freedom of movement of those involved in the corporate culture.

5

What Can We Learn From Others?

Let us imagine a delegation of German politicians sitting in an aeroplane to Amsterdam in the spring of 1997. The tables in front of them are piled high with folders containing charts, economic data and information on areas of competence, social attitudes, party traditions and so on. All this valuable, carefully assembled background material implies that they are not really expecting to learn anything from their neighbours because in reality things are far more complicated in Germany than in a small country like Holland.

One can imagine how much they learned from their visit. *Die Zeit* headed its report at the time: 'The Dutch model. The Swedish model. Rudolf Dressler goes to see for himself and returns with the solution – the German model!'

A similar scene could have taken place in a plane to New York or a train to Copenhagen. The serious public debate over possible international models for German reforms stands in remarkable contrast to the apparent reluctance on the part of many politicians to accept a benchmark index. To a large extent this is an act of self-defence. It is a popular pastime to contrast the alleged decline of the German model with the economic successes of other countries, painting an ever blacker picture and claiming that the political elite in Germany is incapable of making fundamental reforms.

In their book *The Price of Equality: How Germany Lost the Chance of Globalisation*, published in 1998, two journalists, Klaus

Methfessel and Jörg Winterberg, worked with the local rankings published by respected bodies such as the Heritage Foundation, the Fraser Institute and the World Economic Forum. They all predict that in the coming years German incomes will take a dive, compared with those of other countries. Out of 115 countries analysed by the Fraser Institute, Germany was in 25th place, close to Argentina, Bolivia and Chile. The reasons were excessive state spending, excessively high rates of taxation and an overly generous welfare system, which together with an inflexible labour market were responsible for a record level of unemployment.

However, in 1998 it also became clear how little reliability could be placed on such rankings. A striking fact is that in all such lists the Asian states come off far better than Germany. A year earlier they were the lodestars in the economic firmament. And what about today? In the early 1990s the USA was on its way down and Japan was the superpower. And what about today? There is no better evidence of the limited value of comparative performance tables than that afforded by the Asian crisis. That crisis made it clear that what we need is not rankings but carefully compiled long-term benchmark indices that enable us to learn from our shared experience. In the meantime, it is generally accepted that it is not over-regulation *inter alia* that is responsible for the crisis in the states of South-East Asia but the weakness of the regulatory agencies and of political institutions – witness the failure of the supervisory function of the banks in most of the boom states.

Then it was suddenly discovered that the laws of economics had not been nullified in Asia but that as the 'tiger economies' made up ground on the West, so their growth slowed down and their social problems became more pressing. In Indonesia the political and social disturbances of 1998, which led to the resignation of President Suharto, made abundantly clear that the importance of a stable democracy and properly functioning welfare mechanisms for sustained economic development had been grossly underestimated.

Commentators have since come to realize that nepotism and the endemic belief that the function of the economy is first and foremost to consolidate the power of the ruling elite, and only then to attend to the well-being of the people as a whole, were primary factors in the crises that befell South Korea, Malaysia, Thailand, China and Indonesia. To reconcile the primacy of the economy with the social and material needs of the population at large is an enormous challenge for these countries. The days of an hypnotic fascination with the Asian model have gone. In consequence, the growing discrepancy between the ineluctable advance of economic and technological change on the one hand, and the far more sluggish attempts by political and social institutions to adapt to the changed circumstances on the other, has become ever more clearly visible.

At the centre of most analyses of the causes of the Asian crisis, and of the international consequences which may continue to flow from it, stands Japan. It is no coincidence that the debate being carried on there has similarities to that in Germany. An extremely successful export economy is suffering from a chronic lack of domestic demand, a large national debt and dangerous imbalances in public finances. On the heels of a punctured 'soap-bubble economy' fed by speculators comes a debate on how to break the log-jam of necessary reforms, a debate which has many parallels to that taking place in Germany. When, a year after it broke, the Asian crisis reached another climax in the summer of 1998, Japan, once a respected icon, seemed to be caught between a rock and a hard place. In spite of massive government intervention, Japanese gross domestic product recorded minus growth, the Nikkei index plummeted and foreign investment came to a halt. Close observers of the Japanese scene, it must be added, were less surprised than those who before the crisis were putting the Japanese model at the top of the international rankings.

Profound changes are taking place, in the German production model as in the Japanese. Some of these changes are obvious, others only become apparent when one looks more closely. We are facing technological challenges which require new control mechanisms. The Japanese, too, cannot achieve much more with their industrial policies of the 1970s. There is a moral in this. The secret of economic success lies not in industrial policy but in a pattern of social organization that makes it possible to react flexibly to opportunities, problems and challenges.

Everywhere the vital question is whether the state is giving the maximum possible scope to individuals and enterprises to adapt to the pressure for innovation, to adjust to the need for new qualifications and to the bewildering changes in organizational forms and patterns of work, and whether the system for balancing rival interests is sufficiently flexible to be able to produce immediate responses to the questions being posed in social policy, employment policy and economic policy. In 1998 a study was made of the situation in New Zealand, Austria and the USA, which came to the clear conclusion that none of these countries, where the employment climate was clearly more favourable than in Germany through the 1990s, has a blue-print that can simply be transferred to other countries. A second conclusion was equally clear, namely that all three countries studied had had the courage to embark on fundamental reforms in the labour market, in their social policies and in the modernization of the state as a whole.

The Value of Consensus

One model that was eagerly discussed in Germany in 1997 proved not only that such a system could be sustained by a consensus of social forces but also that in given circumstances it could be suitably adopted elsewhere. This is the model evolved in the Netherlands, which at the beginning of the 1980s still operated on an obsolete system of an overstretched welfare state but which has since introduced a thoroughgoing modernization programme. It is particularly instructive to compare the Netherlands with New Zealand, two states often mentioned in the same breath but which have totally different philosophies. Whereas the Netherlands aimed at a social consensus and took a long view, the catastrophic situation in New Zealand cost three political generations their heads, and devastated society. New Zealand has the highest rate of juvenile suicides in the world.

By 1996 the Netherlands had modernized its welfare state, and its so-called 'Polder Model' promised everything that Germany seemed to have lost – consensus and co-operation, with pragmatic cuts in welfare benefits without threatening the welfare model itself. The economy was flourishing. Between 1983 and 1997 unemployment fell from 12 to 5.2 per cent, and in the first half of the 1990s alone one million new jobs were created. This much-quoted 'employment miracle' was mirrored by a huge increase in flexible working. From 1974 to 1995 a growth in the Netherlands economy of 1 per cent produced on average a 0.41 per cent increase in employment. In the USA the figure is 0.75 per cent, in Western Germany a mere 0.23 per cent – though one must remember that in Germany it has long been accepted that only from 2.5 per cent upwards does growth have an effect on employment.

For a long while local councils in Germany watched in astonishment the modernization of local government in the Dutch town of Tilburg, for example, while police and social workers argued for over twenty years about whether the Dutch method of handling the drugs problem could be adopted in Germany. Now, however, it is the success of Dutch economic and social policies that dominates the discussion. The supreme moment of public recognition came with the award of the Carl Bertelsmann Prize to the 'Foundation for Work' in 1997, and the country is justifiably proud of the success of its Polder Model in the economic and employment fields.

Since the Wassenaar Agreement of 1982 between government, employers and workers, the Netherlands had had no comprehensive master plan for the reform of its economic, social and employment policies. There was only a patchwork of reforms – a set of independent measures, the one only occasionally related to the other, which had, however, somehow fused over a period of fifteen years into a kind of system that had previously been hardly recognizable as such. Opinions in Germany over what could be learnt from the Dutch were therefore divided, and a euphoric demand for deregulation of the labour market and permanent wage restraint was met by a critical assessment which insisted on pointing to suspect statistics and the none too encouraging overall state of the Dutch economy.

On this last point – the way the Netherlands calculates its unemployment figures does indeed produce a flattering picture (though the same could be said of many other countries as well, including Germany). Concealed sources push official figures higher, and the OECD put the total in 1996 at 27.1 per cent – which includes highly subsidized jobs, work-creation schemes and other forms of organized exclusion from the standard labour market. Using the same method of computation, one arrives at a figure for Germany of 22 per cent, which takes account of the massive interventions in the eastern territories since reunification.

An important background consideration in the Netherlands is the extensive claims on disability insurance made in the 1970s and 1980s. With the approval of employers and unions, disabled men and women as young as 30 and 40 would be not directly dismissed but pensioned off as disabled. Although this practice has been frowned upon and the numbers have since been radically reduced, it was still reckoned in 1997 that one Dutchman in seven of working age was classed as 'disabled'.

In total, according to the most extensive figures available, one-third of all Dutch people of working age were excluded from the labour market in 1997: in all, 930,000, over 10 per cent, were receiving welfare cheques from sources independent of the un-employment statistics, although in all other European countries they would be counted as unemployed. A total of 890,000 were recorded as permanently unemployable, and another 275,000 took early retirement. Improvements in the employment situation have been registered above all in the categories of older workers and young people, while the unemployment figure for ethnic minor-ities is still considerably higher than in Germany. All this costs a great deal of money. Total deductions from wages and salaries for social security purposes start at 32 per cent for the lowest wage-earners and, apart from Belgium, Italy and Greece, are the highest in the European Union.

But in the Netherlands too people are beginning to take a more critical view of the situation, especially in view of the gloomy growth rate forecasts being made for the end of the century. In the issue of *Die Zeit* for 20 May 1998, Willem Wansink, Nether-lands correspondent, posed the anxious question: 'Will Holland become the Hong Kong of Europe?' If growth declines, says Wansink, in a colourful image, 'all the social shipwrecks will become visible that have collected in the estuary of the Rhine'.

In September 1997 the McKinsey Global Institute and the Max Geldens Foundation for Societal Renewal, based in Holland, published the results of their investigation into the economic performance of the Netherlands. They concluded that the Dutch economy had made up a considerable proportion of the employ-ment losses it had undergone in the 1970s and 1980s. An inter-national comparison of data on production, employment and productivity, however, revealed that there were weak spots in growth and employment in rapidly expanding areas such as the software industry. Here the workers' contribution is four times higher per head in the USA than in the Netherlands. Where it was possible to make up deficits, it was always at the expense of lower-qualified workers. McKinsey and Geldens considered a 15 per cent increase in production and a million new jobs to be possible. In return, barriers of the kind with which we have become familiar in Germany must be broken down – long-drawn-out procedures for granting permissions, inadequate competitive opportunities in growth industries, inflexible labour laws and compensation regulations, an inability to adjust to new circumstances on the part of employers' organizations.

On the other hand, enthusiastic economists and employers' representatives who saw in the 'Polder Model' the perfect prescription for an ailing German economy, had in general only a very restricted view of what its success factors actually were. Pivotal in their eyes was wage restraint on the part of the workers, which the unions had come to accept in the course of the negotiations that led them and the employers to sign the Wassenaar Agreement in 1982. Between 1985 and 1995 the annual nominal wage increase was only 2.6 per cent, a figure only slightly above the rate of inflation.

To be sure, moderate wage increases without a fall in economic demand did play an important part, but only after the rush to make up lost ground in the 1990s after years of moderation and economic growth had failed to materialize is it possible to talk of a definite political decision. From 1991 to 1994 real wage costs in Germany, including wage-added costs, rose by 4.1 per cent, only marginally higher than the 3.9 per cent in the Netherlands.

With extremely low average working hours in the Netherlands, wage differentials are so small that economists of the old school must have found themselves wondering whether this ought not inevitably to have had negative consequences for the employment situation. According to this logic, and to the arguments of the employers, the extremely low number of man-hours worked in the Netherlands is bound to have a disastrous effect on the performance of the economy. In 1997 Günther Schmid, of the Wissenschaftszentrum in Berlin, asked: 'Has the dramatic growth rate of the Netherlands declined as a result of its radical redistribution of incomes and labour, as received Neoclassical wisdom has it and as classical Keynesianism would predict? Far from it. The Netherlands exhibits the same dynamic growth as the USA.'

A number of the central features of the Polder Model correspond to projects which have been discussed in Germany time and again over the last fifteen years. But whereas the Dutch made a determined thrust, one reform following on the heels of another, with a willingness to innovate and experiment, Germany has been held back by its obsession with finding absolute and permanent solutions. The degree of pragmatism displayed by the Social Democrats in the Dutch parliament in considering, despite ideological opposition from within their own party, the possibility of free market initiatives and of cuts in the welfare system, is quite extraordinary. This pragmatism was facilitated by the fact that many of the new laws passed were covered by the concept of so-called 'sunset legislation', i.e. laws, checked for their efficacy but also for their possible incidental effects, which may cease to be valid after a given period. What may seem appropriate today may turn out to be inappropriate tomorrow. This pragmatic approach gives the Dutch a flexibility over reforms which Germany still lacks.

Negotiation and consensus are at the root of the Dutch way of doing things. The opposing parties are well aware of each other's weaknesses. In the last twenty years no party has ever succeeded in winning more than 25 per cent of the votes, and trade-union membership stands at 26 per cent. Try as they might, no one institution had any hope of getting its way without the help of others, which means that everything has to be done through debate and discussion. In the same spirit, institutions that had been devoted to the democratic principle of policy-making by consensus were not done away with but modernized. If the parties, the unions and the employers wish to push their own proposals through, they have to have recourse to fora such as the Social and Economic Advisory Committee or the Planning Bureau, bodies on which outside experts also sit. This format proved more than adequate to secure the acceptance of a great variety of hitherto contentious experiments for change. It also proved a way for an institution like the social democratic Dutch Labour Party to settle controversial debates within the party itself.

This is perhaps the most important lesson that the Dutch model has to teach us. Here we find a clear answer to the question of how institutions can be embedded in an economy which can enhance a country's competitiveness in world markets without incurring excessive welfare costs. A survey of the various politico-economic models in the world concluded that both Germany and the Netherlands are examples, with certain differing features, of a consensus model which is a highly efficient alternative to the liberal Anglo-American model. This was the conclusion reached in 1997 in 'Challenging Neighbours', an exhaustive comparative study undertaken by the Netherlands Bureau for Economic Policy Analysis. 'Whereas Germany, when the market fails, reacts by introducing stricter controls,' concluded the report, 'the Netherlands relies on negotiation, co-operation and consensus.'

The Dutch welfare state is engaged in a search for a new balance between economic competitiveness, the principle of welfare and gainful employment (including a new pattern of work-sharing within the family). The growing pressure exerted by the global economy has not provoked the Netherlands to go down the slippery path of American welfare capitalism. Instead it is evolving a combination of co-operative, efficient, high-quality industrial production with flexible working practices and social security. Its strength lies in the high degree of decentralization facilitated by the co-operation model, with all sides sharing responsibility for the conclusions arrived at.

The direct responsibilities of the Social and Economic Advisory Council and the Employment Foundation are not wide. Critical, however, is their arrival at a common interpretation of the problems under discussion, which facilitates consensus and co-operation in decentralized bodies also. These two organizations belong to the comprehensive network of negotiating bodies which not only fulfil a socio-economic function – agreements on wages policy represent only one facet of its activities – but which also play a part in co-operation between factories, in the dissemination of knowledge and in the encouragement of innovation. As a result, the Dutch economy has developed into a network economy with a broad spread of institutions which, in the form of foundations, for instance, give financial and other support to small and medium-sized businesses and newly founded companies, and organize the transfer of knowledge. One product of this system has been a considerable increase in the flexibility of small businesses. Dutch suppliers organized in network systems of this kind have in the meantime outstripped those in other countries in terms of flexibility and quality.

The quality of these new jobs is beyond dispute. This is not casual work in McDonalds or anything of that nature. Two-thirds of the part-time workers in the Netherlands have had qualified training of one kind or another, which suggests that at least a substantial proportion of these jobs demand a specific skill. The more dynamic and technologically progressive a particular sector, the greater the use made of flexible working practices among more highly skilled personnel as well as others. Half the new vacancies created in the 1990s were in the flourishing field of part-time work.

Disapproval of such jobs, which is gradually disappearing in Germany, is unknown in Holland. Contrary to what is widely assumed, however, the Dutch labour market has not been deregulated but rather 'de-institutionalized' – that is to say, traditional full-time working has been replaced by a part-time model, without creating a mass of jobs that offer no guarantee of security. Rather, the constant mutual feedback between flexible business structures and flexible labour markets guarantees a higher elasticity of growth and employment.

But the growing number of part-time workers and workers on temporary loan also coincides, from the trade unions' point of view, with the wishes of the employees themselves, while to categorize part-time work as 'insecure' is quite unjustified, since such employees enjoy the protection of employment law and all the institutionalized benefits of the social security system. In a number of other areas, such as terms of severance and resignation, or a minimum wage for adults, there have been occasional initiatives over the years, but there has been no comprehensive deregulation. Only since the mid-1990s has there been something of a return to such policies.

Yet since the beginning of the 1970s – reaching its height in the 1980s – the proportion of part-time employees in the Netherlands rose from 5 to 35 per cent, and in the case of women from 15 to 65 per cent. No other OECD country can match this. In Germany the figure is a mere 18 per cent overall, with that for men standing at as little as 3 per cent. At the same time one cannot deny that the high rate of part-time working in the Netherlands has a number of snags. Around a third of such employees work fewer than ten hours a week, and employment protection laws often do not apply fully to mini-jobs like these – though this does not leave the way open for a 'hire and fire' policy. Also, such employees are finding it increasingly difficult to be accepted into official pension schemes.

All in all, one may see the rising employment figures in the Netherlands as in essence the product of a huge redistribution of labour, which includes a corresponding redistribution of incomes. However, this only reduces the attractiveness of the Polder Model for those who insist on clinging to the old model of full-time employment and maintain that this is the only way to guarantee social security and status.

But if one takes the view that a part-time job is better than none, and if one is prepared to give up an exclusive demand for full-time working, the situation looks different. In the Netherlands provision for the social security of unemployed workers is taken generously into account against their earnings when they accept a part-time job. Moreover, a man or woman who works fewer than ten hours a week is also entitled to unemployment benefit as long as he or she is an active job-seeker. This 'top-up system' removes the part-time worker's fear of not receiving an adequate retirement pension.

Since 1982 the system has also applied to those who have renounced their claim to a full-time job and declared their willingness to accept any work that might be offered them. A familiar case in point is that of unemployed teachers who work as tourist guides in Amsterdam. Nowhere in the Netherlands has this scheme caused howls of indignation.

America – Model or Myth?

For years the United States has been the point of reference in discussions of economic and employment policies. In the mid-1980s the American economy looked to be ailing, but since May 1998, when unemployment fell to 4.8 per cent, the lowest figure for twenty-four years, its performance has attracted only superlatives. In 1997 alone it produced 3.2 million new jobs. At the 1998 G7 summit President Clinton held up the USA as an example to all slack economies, and Vice-President Al Gore waxed eloquent over a 'Tiger Woods economy' – an allusion to the young American golfer who went from one success to another in the 1990s. Low unemployment and low inflation seem to have become standard for the USA. Whereas in the 1980s the US economy looked to be at the bottom of the league of industrialized nations as far as competitiveness was concerned, the 'German sickness' now provoked a smug sense of *Schadenfreude*, and the remarkable US employment statistics had a powerful influence on the course of discussions in Germany.

Opinions in Germany differed over how to judge this success in terms of the quality of the new jobs created, and whether,

considering the polarizing effects it had on society, it was justifiable
to talk of a 'model' at all. At all events it is clear that the American labour market has always recovered from crises more quickly
than the German, where core unemployment has risen step by
step. According to figures from the OECD, long-term unemployment in the USA stands at 9.7 per cent, far lower than the 48.3
per cent for the whole of Germany today.

All the forecasts point to a marked rise in employment in the
USA until the end of the twentieth century – a rise apparently
not dependent on upwards or downwards movements of the
economy but to reflect long-term capacity. Trends which in
Germany take some time to become established – the increasing
number of female workers, for instance, or the rapid growth of
the service sector, which is responsible for every second newly
created job in America – move very much faster in the USA. Yet
throughout the whole period of the American 'employment
miracle' economic growth in the USA was not substantially higher
than in Germany. But in America every additional percentage
point of gross domestic product produces 0.64 million new jobs,
whereas to achieve the same result in Germany would require a
growth rate seven times as large. And the myth that the majority
of these new jobs in America are for poorly qualified workers in
the lowest-paid sectors has long since been disproved.

There are many indications that Germany can learn from American experience in employment policy, above all in the question
of higher flexibility at the lower end of the labour market. I am
well aware that this is a taboo subject. It is true that the growth
of job opportunities in the USA has had negative consequences,
especially as regards job security. These are two sides of the same
coin. Because of the enormous fluctuations in the labour market,
there is little opportunity for unemployment to become structurally established. But one reason for this is the low degree of
protection against summary dismissal. There are few regulations
providing, say, for discussions with staff representatives in the case
of dismissal, hardly any welfare provisions and no restrictions on
the time limitations of short-term contracts.

This also applies to better-paid jobs. At the beginning of 1998
the Center for National Policy in Washington found that the
index that measures the number of jobs without pension rights
or sickness and unemployment insurance had fallen, and was
continuing to do so. The advantages of flexibility, with the wholly

inadequate social protection measures that accompany them, entail social costs that no party in Germany could or would be prepared to pay.

One has to see this development against a background of fundamentally different conditions as concerns occupational expectations and individual careers. In the USA the overwhelming majority of workers do not expect to stay in one job longer than five years. Polls have shown that many of those content to work under such flexible conditions would actually resent having their hands tied by a firm wage agreement negotiated by a trade union. However, there are also signs of a growing disintegration, especially in the middle echelons.

Another point is the immense range of incomes, which, in combination with an expansive monetary policy, many experts agree has greatly contributed to the success of America's employment policies. But this too resulted in a dangerous social polarization which also affected the middle echelons. To be sure, in 1997, thanks to a wage hike of 3.4 per cent in real terms, the fall in real wages was halted, but this only brought the figure back to that of 1989. And running side by side with this, the range of incomes has been widening dramatically since 1979, not only between the highest and lowest incomes but also between those in the highest and those in the middle-income bracket.

Put bluntly, this means that flexibility at the lower end of the labour market is being paid for, at least in part, by economic and social costs which Germany certainly could not afford. On the question of economic development, those who point to the benefits of deregulation and low wages for the labour market would be well advised to think again. In discussions on the position of the service industries, the low-wage option may make social and economic sense. But in the context of industrial productivity and in the company-based service sector, this broad wage-spread, in the USA and elsewhere, has not only had positive effects but has at times been actually counter-productive. Thus, where productivity rose by 38 per cent from 1980 to 1994, in the USA it rose by only 17 per cent. Not for nothing has a heated argument been raging in recent years over the need to raise the standards of school education, vocational training and adult education. At the present time 30 per cent of Americans leave school without being able to read or write. In the eyes of many experts the so-called dual system of vocational training still remains the best model.

In spite of these ambiguous conclusions there are still things Germany can learn from the American model. But they do not lie so much in the area of rigid deregulation in the labour market, or of cutting the period of entitlement to unemployment and social security benefits. Of greater relevance is the basic philosophy of employment policy, which raises social issues which we in Germany need to confront today. In addition to this, the social democratic countries of Europe – against a background of more fully developed social security systems and stronger protection from employment legislation – are following the same path in employment policy as the USA, a 'third way' between the American model and the West European welfare state.

Germany, however, lacks that overall conception which would clinch the issue – not something to help us put across unpopular measures but a new model, a positive and proactive initiative to introduce flexibility into the labour market. Globalization will force us to confront this question, whether we like it or not.

In August 1996, on signing the welfare reform bill, President Clinton announced a fundamental change of direction in the philosophy of the welfare state which has nowhere been more radically put into practice than in the USA – a philosophy which in essence underlies the principles of New Labour in the UK and of the policies being pursued by the Netherlands and by Denmark, among others. From now on, said Clinton, America's answer to the unremitting social challenge of unemployment will no longer be based on the never-ending 'welfare spiral' but on the dignity and ethic of individual work. 'Today,' said the President, 'we are putting into effect an historical change which will enable welfare to again become what it was meant to be – not a way of life but a second chance.'

The allegation that this was an effective way of concealing radical cuts is only partly true. America has introduced a number of measures which increase the interchangeability between the welfare system and the labour market. It is true that, from the German point of view, the enormous pressure put on the unemployed and those on welfare to go into work is one of the more undesirable features of the American system. But the argument over whether any job is better than none has already reached European shores. We live in a society in which we feel obliged to work, not only because the state assumes that this is so and holds us in the grip of this mentality, but also because it corresponds to a fundamental need in us. For this reason, and not only on grounds of cost, we cannot afford, morally, to continue to support the unemployed for ever without offering them a real opportunity to earn a living.

As to the question of the role the welfare state can and should play in the future, the left wing has as yet produced no plan of action. Critics of the USA point out how depressing it must be for a young person starting in work to have to reckon on being unemployed again twelve months later. But such critics must face the question whether that is not better than having to tell applicants for unemployment benefit in Germany that in all probability they will in a year's time still be dependent on hand-outs from the working society from which they are excluded. It is easy to sneer at America with remarks such as 'once a worker in a hamburger joint, always a worker in a hamburger joint'. But for many, such jobs are the way, or the way back, into a genuine career. The *Süddeutsche Zeitung* said on 5 August 1997: 'If one is talking about a miracle, then it did not take place in America but in Germany. For here the miracle is that having no job at all appears to be more highly prized than having a job at McDonalds.'

It is essential, of course, that we find a solution proper to the German situation, so that those who warn us of the 'working poor' syndrome do not carry the day. In Germany the emphasis will be rather on lowering labour costs, especially at the lower end of the labour market – in other words, a spread of labour costs instead of a polarization of wages. This is the thought behind the SPD's proposal to subsidize added wage costs at the lower end of the income scale. This strikes at the heart of the debate on the 'joint wage'. One of the most important political topics in Germany today is how to restore to the under-qualified and the long-term unemployed the hope of regaining their dignity and pride through work. Today's army of unemployed will continue to lack confidence in the state and in politics until it becomes evident that the politicians responsible for economic and employment policy genuinely have their interests at heart.

With his campaign 'to end welfare as we know it', President Clinton latched on to a widespread attitude in the population as a whole. Hitherto, support for programmes identified with the concept of 'welfare' had been steadily crumbling, while approval of social security programmes providing for retirement pensions funded by contributions remained relatively high. In 1996 the

Personal Responsibility and Work Opportunity Act, the central welfare scheme for poor families, was abolished and replaced by short-term assistance for single mothers, aimed at returning them as quickly as possible to gainful employment.

American employment policy mirrors a nationwide debate on the causes of poverty and the ways of dealing with it. In signing the reform measures of 1996 into law, President Clinton described them as helping to put an end to the terrible sense of isolation from the rest of society felt by the poor, and giving them the chance to rejoin 'mainstream America'. Only through the sweat of one's brow can one carve out for oneself a place in society.

This is a view that has been vigorously propounded since the 1980s by conservative academics such as Charles Murray and Lawrence Mead. At the centre of their argument, which is widely accepted throughout American society, stands the principle that welfare policy is itself the cause of unemployment and the slide into poverty. Welfare, according to Murray and Mead, disguises the individual's feelings of guilt at finding himself in such a desperate plight, creates a state of permanent dependence on hand-outs and results in dysfunctional behaviour on the part of those on welfare. Nothing is easier and more natural to explain than the conduct of those who prefer to accept generous welfare cheques to taking some badly paid job. It is the perfectly understandable reaction of people who have decided on common-sense economic grounds to maximize their quality of life. Whole groups of the population are enabled with the help of welfare to adopt a lifestyle far removed from social reality, a lifestyle they subsequently find it almost impossible to give up.

Only a new social contract with the state, based on the principle of reciprocal service, this argument concludes, can integrate unemployed adults into a society whose ethos is dominated by the work ethic. It is then the duty of the state to lay down standards of procedure to help individuals in their return to gainful employment by providing social amenities such as kindergartens and crèches.

In Germany, too, people are coming to realize that economic logic does not stop at those on welfare. But the debate is proceeding cautiously, by fits and starts, even though some social scientists are already beginning to talk of a poverty trap which the welfare system sets for those who prefer to accept state hand-outs to taking low-paid work, and who, after a period of dequalification and demotivation, later find themselves unable to reverse their decision.

Many local authorities in Germany have therefore started to convert welfare into a system in which applicants are offered jobs and opportunities for training, including the planning of an entire career, where appropriate, leading eventually to a full-time job in the open labour market. Furthermore, the principle of scrutinizing institutions to see whether they are encouraging or hindering the growth of employment has been extended to cover matters such as security of tenure and protection from unlawful dismissal. The SPD plans to repeal a number of the previous government's uncoordinated amendments to the law governing unlawful dismissal and replace them with considered proposals as to how one can make more systematic and consistent use of, for example, temporary contracts of employment as a means of helping the unemployed to get back into work.

There is a clear trend in the USA to let all other social and political measures take second place to attempts at rapid reintegration into the labour market. Most of the states in the union have started to cut back on measures designed, for instance, to promote the gaining of qualifications, in favour of a more direct involvement in the mechanisms of the labour market. This is also linked to the fact that, among other things, the cost of immediate employment measures is less than that of training programmes. It is also consistent with the whole philosophy of the labour market. According to federal statistics, in 1997 25 per cent of welfare recipients throughout the country had accepted jobs; in 2000 the figure is expected to rise to 40 per cent, and in 2002 to 50 per cent. The individual states may require men and women on welfare to work twenty hours a week, after two months, to help pay off their benefits.

To be entitled to financial support, men and women alike must, within this framework, accept subsidized or unsubsidized private positions, job-induction courses or practical training. Receipt of welfare is limited to a period of five years in the life of each individual. After two years, all receivers of welfare have their support withdrawn and are expected to take up employment. Mothers of children over three years of age are also required as a rule to 'earn' their hand-outs by working twenty hours a week.

This is only a summary sketch of American welfare and employment policy. But it quickly becomes clear that their reform of welfare policy is based on one logical premise, namely that radical withdrawal of benefits creates unwelcome material pressure, which in return accelerates a return to employment. This material pressure is then intensified by a psychological pressure emanating from the public debate over the individual's obligations to society. The underlying philosophy might be described as 'social insecurity as a goad to progress'.

From a German point of view such economic and social pressure is no doubt regarded as inhuman. But it is not in our interests to refuse to discuss these American policies, for the measures taken in America to set the rights of the individual in society against the individual's obligations to that society reveal remarkable parallels to what is being discussed in Germany.

Take, for instance, President Clinton's dramatic raising of the rate of negative income tax, which will be used to top up low incomes. As a result low wage earners have a higher income than before, in spite of lower net wages. The terminology used in American legislation on social and employment policy is highly revealing. Instead of the term 'welfare', which for the majority of people had become like a red rag to a bull, implying idleness and cadging, we find words like 'workfare' and 'learnfare'.

In Germany we need to develop our own new philosophy of the welfare state. The development of complex national insurance schemes can only ever take place in terms of what is feasible. But our objective is clear, and, for all its differences, our position is in reality very close to that of the Americans, namely that we can no longer afford to go on supporting long-term unemployment instead of financing employment. We also need a higher degree of crossover between the welfare system and the labour market, so that we can close the poverty trap. American experience in these matters can be expected to have a lasting influence on the German domestic debate.

One final observation on the subject of America as model and as myth. In other, more general areas than that of employment, we should not blind ourselves to what we can learn from the United States. Despite all the criticisms one can make of the social consequences of a free market economy, the basic attractiveness of the American system lies in its openness to individual innovations and organizational reforms. The root of the German problem is psychological – envy of others' success, suspicion of both neighbours and outsiders, intolerance towards trouble-makers and fault-finders. The most important lesson we can learn from America is not to greet someone who has failed with spiteful scorn but to give them a second chance. Despite their aggressive competitive spirit, the Americans also show team spirit, not agonizing endlessly over their problems but facing up to them with imagination and determination.

In Germany, by contrast, we are scarcely able to conceive of a situation in which a problem may also be an exciting challenge, and from the solution of which we might derive a sense of enjoyment. The American sociologist Audretsch concluded in 1996 that genuine innovations only arise when people think unconventional thoughts and act on them. Germany has not recognized the fact that its economic problems constitute not a recession but a structural crisis, and that a structural crisis cannot be solved from within the existing structures. Germany must change from being an economy focused on production to one based on ideas and knowledge. This is a task that will not be successfully achieved without a goodly portion of optimism and enterprise.

6

New Paths to Growth and Full Employment

In a policy statement published in March 1998 the management committee of the Friedrich Ebert Foundation demanded 'a more radical approach in dealing with the *réalités*'. In other words, the Foundation was looking for an end to the ideological debates that have plagued us for so long, in particular the endless toing and froing between demand-side and supply-side economics.

This argument has been carried on in both the Christian Democrat and the Social Democrat camps. But the perpetual squabbling between supply-side policies aimed at reducing wage costs and Keynesian demand-oriented formulae aimed at raising wage rates – both in the name of full employment – has contributed little towards solving the problem. On the one hand, supply-side doctrines would require settling on employment costs matched by a 'balanced wage' that would clear the labour market. But wages are not just a cost factor for the employer – they provide the income and family budget of the employee. On the other hand, the demand effect of every wage rise peters out if it is eaten up by the employer's rising added costs and if there is no change in the global competitive situation and the economic structure. Most people have long since turned away from the idea of Keynesian panaceas that will work overnight. The situation is far more complicated.

There are industries in which one could go so far as to say that there is no limit to how expensive employment can be because there is no limit to how productive and innovative it can be.

Market leadership and innovations do not come cheap. On the other hand, low-qualified jobs fall victim to the competitive pressure of productivity, so that there are bound to be industries which can no longer meet the normal wage bill, let alone the wage-added costs. Even traditional industries that manufacture goods that can be produced anywhere in the world will feel the goad of productivity – that is to say, the constant pressure on costs and wages. Such matters can be settled by organizational measures, but it will continue to be at the expense of jobs.

Another frequent subject of argument, much of it conducted in ideological terms, is that of cut-backs in subsidies. In recent years this discussion has always tended to become distorted by the classic example of the mining industry. The fact is that in the long run subsidies always come back to haunt the subsidizer, above all because they strengthen lobbies, consolidate private interests and have a tendency to make themselves permanent and put themselves beyond criticism. In January 1997 the Institute for World Economy in Kiel put the total of subsidies – including those from the federal government, the *Länder*, local authorities and the European Union – at almost 300 billion marks per year. Since 1982 a generous policy of subsidies and state-funded programmes was firmly established as part of the conservative government's interventionist policies. With a national rate of almost half of gross domestic product, few today still remember that at the time of the so-called 'change of direction' announced by the conservative government in 1981–2, an alarming figure of 50 per cent was kept for dealing with communism.

Cut-backs in subsidies must be aimed at supporting structural change. The German coal industry offers an instructive example. The aim is not to use subsidies to prop up an old and no longer sustainable industry in its traditional structures, but to embark on a thoroughgoing regional, technological and economic reform of these structures that will also have the confidence of the workforce. Hardly any other industry has handled this development so quickly and so efficiently as the mining industry. If all those in receipt of subsidies had put forward a comparable plan for their repayment, as the coal industry agreed with the federal government and the *Land* of North-Rhine-Westphalia, the state would have saved up to 100 billion marks.

Indeed, new and innovative industries, and above all founders of new businesses, are barely affected by regional subsidies. The industrial policies of the 1970s are no longer relevant. According to the findings of the Fraunhofer Institute for Systems Technology and Innovation Research, the key to innovative developments in areas such as macro-systems technology and the production logistics of marketing products and services lies with small and medium-sized companies, which need a completely new kind of economic policy. Programmes promoting innovation and expansion in smaller companies need to be more clearly defined and better co-ordinated. The European Union, the federal government and the *Länder* provide together more than 600 support programmes, usually with small budgets, distributed on the so-called 'garden sprinkler' principle – which, however, has not had the effect of making the individual programmes more accessible to smaller companies. Even with the twenty most important promotional programmes it is hardly possible to assess their success without the help of an outside adviser. And nobody knows how much money has been wasted in the labyrinthine bureaucracy of the state and the European Union. Only where the effectiveness and transparency of the support is improved is there a comparable improvement in performance.

Subsidies should therefore be granted on a competitive basis, with awards being given to the best suggestions. Any investment of economic effort which does not involve a fundamentally different attitude on our part towards competition, risk and the creation of new businesses, is doomed to failure. We need a 'supply-side economics of the left'. Modern economic policy has the responsibility for improving conditions for investment, innovation and employment, and for combining economic dynamism with the creation of new jobs. A committee of the Friedrich Ebert Foundation identified in 1998 three areas in which such a policy could help to overcome blockages and obstacles – frictions in the innovation system, the removal of discrepancies in the compatibilization of qualifications, and inadequacies in the services provided by the public sector.

Indeed, our approach to innovation has long been more important than labour costs, and the viability of our society depends on our ability to innovate and on the international competitiveness of our technologically highly advanced economy. A high-tech industrial and service provider such as Germany will only increase its competitive opportunities in world markets if innovative products are developed for new markets and supplied through intelligent processes – high-tech products, in which at least 5 per cent of turnover is invested in research and development.

There is, of course, no virtue in plunging into the competitive high-tech world without taking account of the structures already in existence. An economy's ability to innovate does not rest on a narrow ideology such as that based on the assumption that a man who can make the world's most efficient microchip, for example, will always lead the field. Half of all innovations between now and the year 2020 are expected to be in the chemical industry, a traditional branch of industry well represented in North-Rhine-Westphalia. The innovations that have taken place in the automobile industry over recent years could well be characterized as 'spontaneous investments'. Such examples show that the greatest opportunities lie not in a frantic attempt to make up for lost ground in the most modern technologies but in faster feedback between the technologies of the future and the historical areas of technological and economic strength.

One problem that remains is that an increase in the rate of innovation has not yet manifested itself on the labour market. In fact, in the 1990s employment in the technological and research-intensive industries in Germany fell rather than rose. This gives the term 'innovation blockage' a totally new meaning. To the Social Democrats, an innovation is only an innovation when it provides work security and creates new jobs. Innovation is not just new technology but also the creation of new products, new markets and new models, especially in the service industries. Only when more intelligence has gone into a product does it escape from the price race and make a contribution to the higher net product which every country with high wage costs needs.

An invention becomes an innovation only if it finds extensive application. As a research centre, Germany has acquired a strong position with foreign companies, and with good reason. Their sister enterprises have so far spent 9.5 billion marks on research and development in Germany; they employ some 15 per cent of the men and women engaged in research and development in the country, and in terms of the number of businesses in which Japanese equity capital is invested – to quote just one example – Germany is second only to the UK in the European league.

The Friedrich Ebert Foundation concluded in a report that businesses which distribute their research investment over a number of countries ask themselves the following questions: where are the markets of the future in which lessons can be learnt from consumers and an adequate return earned on the substantial outlay involved? Where can these markets most efficiently be served through highly developed production, logistical and supply structures? In which centres, in consequence, will it pay to build up net value? In which countries and regions will attractive markets be coupled with advanced production structures and favourable conditions for research? To these questions I would add another: where is the company prepared to invest in the solution of the problems that have arisen in its own field?

It is particularly vital for concerns operating in world markets to have a firm base which is well equipped in these respects. This is the reason why globalization and regionalization have to go hand in hand. If a particular region, by virtue of its infrastructure, can demonstrate a basic competence in an individual area, funding for research and production will flow in from all over the world. A leading market can thus turn into a highly specialized centre for development and production. The crucial issue is to combine basic research and high technology with developments in the traditionally important branches of German industry.

The economics ministry of North-Rhine-Westphalia has published a discussion paper on the directions which developments in economic and innovative structures might take in the future. One interesting conclusion to which the ministry came was that in the most important fields with a high rate of innovation – data-processing, for example, or biotechnology – the research institutes in North-Rhine-Westphalia were clearly in the lead when compared with the country as a whole. But the technological profile of that *Land* is actually the reverse – that is to say, innovatory activity has been especially marked where research institutes had not expected anything new. The machine tools industry is a case in point.

This is in fact true for the whole of German industry. The ministry's analysis was based on patent statistics, which have only a limited relevance to the development of innovation as a whole. Based on these statistics, for example, the construction industry in Germany would appear highly innovatory. In reality, however, building sites are still dominated by ten traditional trades, with their familiar demarcation disputes and time-wasting procedures. In the Netherlands, on the other hand, the various craftsmen work together as a team. Here are ample opportunities for innovation – not, however, of a technical nature, but in terms of organization, changes in work culture.

The ministry's paper is an important indication of the way the wind is blowing. We must bring science and economics closer together. The heart of the problem is that business tends to assess markets over the short or medium term, with low risk, whereas science thinks in extremely long terms and has as far as possible to take risk out of the equation. We must reverse this logic. The economy has to know what science is capable of achieving; at the same time science has to grasp more quickly what the economy needs. The transfer of knowledge from scientific sources to small and medium-sized businesses leaves a good deal to be desired. Business cannot make an informed approach to science, because what science has to offer usually leaves them out of their depth and there are too few specific information packages available. Science, on the other hand, has little contact with such businesses because the latter often find difficulty in defining precisely what information and research results they require. The same applies to the foundation of new businesses, for which universities and colleges of technology often feel no sense of responsibility. There are in fact great opportunities for colleges to convert research results into marketable products on their campuses. The USA has been doing this for years. There is no reason why we should not do the same.

This would also be a way for the universities to meet the challenges that are facing them. In the coming decade German universities are going to undergo changes comparable only with those that took place in the 1960s and 1970s. We are on the way to a university system with much more competition. Universities are going to have to specialize more and make a deeper mark on society, and as a precondition for this they will have to be given wider scope to decide their own policies and greater financial autonomy.

At the same time we must realize that in practice this autonomy can only really affect about 10 per cent of the available funds: the rest is earmarked for the more-or-less fixed personnel budget, which is not likely to become much more flexible as long as the law governing the remuneration of teachers and other civil servants remains in force. In this connection the future lies rather with the university lecturer on a limited contract, not one with a job for life. Salaries must be geared more closely to performance, and lecturers without doctorates but with experience in industry and administration could adapt many courses to practical needs. Courses must become more career-oriented, and students must be given more encouragement to strike out on their own. In *Länder* under SPD control, universities and other institutions of tertiary education have opened their doors to young artisans, for one of our principles is to put vocational and general education on the same footing.

Our universities must expose themselves to competition. The *Land* of Lower Saxony found it helpful to draw up a league table which gave a comparative evaluation of all the universities. A related and hotly debated subject is that of student fees. But in the course of this debate we overlook the fact that university study in Germany has in recent years become more expensive than it is in America. The majority of students are prepared to pay for their education but only on condition that the money goes directly to their university and to improving their conditions. Measured against the population as a whole, the ratio of students is slightly below average; only in Switzerland and the UK is it lower. German universities offer few attractions to foreign students, and we have been far too dilatory in introducing international entry qualifications.

A capacity to innovate, together with growth in the most important economic fields of the future, both depend more than ever on the availability of qualified men and women. The multimedia industry complained in 1998 that it could have created 17,000 more jobs if only enough suitably qualified graduates had been available. And 75,000 positions were left unfilled. The electronics industry is crying out for applicants.

To some extent this is a result of a long period of consolidation: school-leavers saw a career in manufacturing as a job in a dying industry. But the present-day situation also points to the need for a root-and-branch modernization of the entire German system of further education and training. The North-Rhine-Westphalian project that I discussed earlier in connection with the need for a plan for a co-operative economic policy is also relevant here. It has the support of politicians and unions, and its reform projects tackle the subject at its roots. The short-term objective is to offer every school-leaver who asks for it a place on a training course. Regional conferences which reflect the supply-and-demand situation in respect of apprenticeships more accurately than official statistics also welcome the initiative, and there is a hotline ready to provide information and advice. The system can then be extended by regional computer link-ups which anybody can access – a worker, for example, anxious to see what further training courses are on offer.

In the medium term the North-Rhine-Westphalian plan is a reform proposal aimed at modernizing the dual vocational training system, removing artificial barriers by improving the link between factory or office and educational establishment, adding to the scope of vocational training to take account of rapidly growing new occupations – in the media, for instance – and of technological developments in existing occupations. Thus the number and structure of the available job descriptions still reflects a traditional 'industrial culture'. That 75 per cent of these job descriptions refer to manufacturing is an over-diversification, especially as only 25 per cent of employees actually work in this field. In the service industries the situation is the reverse. We therefore need a faster supply of new job descriptions, while the pattern of existing jobs must be more quickly brought up to date and the way opened for specialization – industrial, professional and regional.

The universality of the new technologies calls for a broad basic education followed by specialization. Nor is it only the most able who need attractive job descriptions – the less gifted also need training courses. We need a wider range of options in our vocational training programmes, including introductory courses and the possibility of giving certificates to those who are not up to a three-year full-time course but who nevertheless can have achieved something useful after two years. Diversification of this kind also makes sense for the more highly gifted. A secondary school pupil training to become a joiner and a sixth-former who has already passed his *Abitur* – his final exam – and is now studying interior design with the intention of becoming an architect make quite different demands on what and how they are taught. The initial educational programme needs to be made more compact, in terms both of content and organization.

A further premise is the provision of good basic training but at the same time regular refresher courses and opportunities for further qualification for all workers, men and women alike. Workers must understand that qualifications offer the best form of protection from unemployment, and employers, for their part, must realize that they can only compete in world markets with a qualified workforce.

Very few companies have a precise idea of what further training their workers require, let alone how this training can be provided. Practical proposals are in short supply, especially in smaller firms. The slogan 'lifelong learning' presupposes that basic training will be followed by further training and by promotion. We need to find ways and means of offering a second chance to young people whose learning capacity and motivation is poor, while at the same time making it possible for ambitious and practically gifted people to develop their talents through further qualifications, especially after they have completed an apprenticeship. We cannot afford to have phases of unemployment – only phases of learning and further learning. Periods of unemployment must be used to prepare for a different occupation, which requires from the beginning a more flexible combination of occupational basic training and a modular system of further courses which can be taken one by one for as long as the individual feels the need and the capability. It is the responsibility of the state to plan in the present for the needs of the future. Our entire education system stands at the crossroads. Its efficiency will be one of the factors that decide whether Germany can compete in international markets.

I am not one of those who join in the general chorus of criticism of our schools – as when a report maintains, for example, that German schoolchildren compare unfavourably with those of other countries in their knowledge of mathematics and science. But it remains a fact that 20 per cent of pupils from secondary schools leave without a qualification that would entitle them to take a vocational training course. Our children also start school later than those of many other countries, and we allow more years to elapse before they reach their *Abitur*. This does not mean that they are the cleverer for that. Textbooks pay too little attention to economics, innovation and technology, the relationship between ecology and economics, independent careers and similar subjects – or at best, the information in such textbooks is out of date.

But the situation gets worse. The power of privilege is creeping over our educational system. Parents have long been paying for their children's education. Two billion marks a year is spent on out-of-school coaching. It is no coincidence that almost one in two pupils receiving coaching comes from a middle-class professional family. Equality of opportunity in education over the country as a whole is a thing of the past. According to the OECD, no industrialized country spends less of its national budget on education than Germany.

We do not need to indulge in ideological debates on what is the best form of school. Comparisons with other countries show that results have nothing to do with systems. What we should be discussing is what society can legitimately expect from our schools, training colleges and universities and what society must offer educational institutions in order for them to live up to these expectations. Educational institutions need more independence and responsibility; in schools, for instance, this would be linked to greater freedom in the appointment of teachers within fixed staff budgets. Schools and colleges must submit to competition and allow their results to be monitored, not only internally within the educational system itself but publicly and by independent bodies.

We need a new concept of education. We are a highly qualified nation but we are slow to adapt and are weighed down by unnecessary knowledge. Investment in curiosity is investment in the future. All our schools should therefore be on the internet. The day will come when our children have to change the world, but we are not showing them how best to put into effect all the knowledge we have. Why should managers, artists or trade-unionists not work part time as teachers in our schools and universities? Our educational system has to be brought into closer contact with society and its needs.

All this shows how widely the concept of innovation and diversification must be interpreted. Interestingly enough, the introduction of innovations in industry has often been linked with flexible working time, worker participation and similar organizational models. The ability to innovate is a question that touches the whole of society, a problem of mentalities and of infrastructures in the state, in administration, in science and throughout our educational system. Knowledge and skill in dealing with speculative technologies must take the place of myths, hesitancy and apprehension.

What, then, are the innovations that will secure the economic future of the Federal Republic of Germany? In the first place we need mental and psychological innovation. We want jobs, but we continue to cling to the romantic notion that we can guarantee prosperity without undergoing permanent technological change. We need a social climate conducive to innovation so that we can more readily participate in technological and social advances. Ability to innovate is more than just technology plus production skills, for in the last analysis it is society that decides on whether social needs are converted into markets.

The scientists of the so-called 'Delphi Project', a broad survey of the technological and scientific needs of the coming century, have attempted to forecast the outlines of social demand in the year 2015. The greatest opportunities are to be found where technological innovations have been spawned by these very opportunities and by the contribution they have made to solving social problems. This applies, for instance, to the combination of media technology and social services, or to new forms of management and work organization. In a poll conducted throughout the EU countries, Canada and the USA, 74 per cent of those asked agreed with the statement, 'Science and technology have made our lives healthier, easier and more comfortable.' On the other hand many of those asked expressed themselves worried by the time it took for paperwork to be dealt with by the authorities.

People have come to see where the risks inherent in technological development lie. The danger is not innovation but missed opportunities. In genetics and biotechnology political policies are often quoted as being to blame for driving innovation and applied research out of Germany. In fact, the state has only converted into rules and regulations the feelings of resentment already shared by many in the population, seeing that as its political obligation. But it is no less the responsibility of the state to break down these feelings and promote a desire for innovation, encourage discussion of the new opportunities and not add to the sense of apprehension over the risks.

A proper framework for the introduction of innovations cannot be created from on high by regulating or deregulating but only by consensus among all the constituent elements in society, not excluding those at regional level. If there is a renaissance of regional economies within globalization, then this will also apply to the style and the instruments of economic policy. Examples from North-Rhine-Westphalia and other *Länder* show that it makes sense to think in terms of a regional economic and structural policy built on co-operation and with an eye on the competitiveness of the locality.

In 1998 the international financial advisers Ernst and Young undertook a comparative study of ten European industrial regions to identify the principal competitive factors at work – innovation, skills, productivity and other items such as institutional structures, regional policies and social consensus. North-Rhine-Westphalia comes out above average in all areas, earning particular commendation for its broad consensus on strategies of modernization, such as that embodied in the project 'Go!' It is here that one can see most clearly what instruments have to be employed to improve the contextual conditions for innovation and employment.

The familiar 'innovation regime' adopted throughout Germany rests on four pillars: established technological strengths in areas such the chemical, motor vehicle and engineering industries; a decentralized system of scientific knowledge; a firm core of skilled workers; and the dual training system. To these, one could add a fifth – the dynamic of the creation of new businesses and a consequent increase in the incidence of structural change.

It must be clear to everybody that fresh work can only come with the establishment of new businesses. Of central state grants and tax concessions a mere 3 per cent accrues to middle-ranking firms – a sign of how little attention has been paid in recent years to the interests of smaller companies. Compared with the other *Länder* of the old West Germany, North-Rhine-Westphalia is short of some 80,000 such companies, around 23,000 of them in skilled trades. If these arrears were made up, 300,000 new jobs would be created.

Under the aegis of the 'Go!' programme, between 300 and 400 million marks a year have been spent since 1996 on supporting the creation of new firms. An original aspect of this programme has been a public relations and marketing campaign addressed to the constituent elements of society itself – families, school, universities, the media – in order to create a culture of enterprise and initiative. Economic policy is, after all, part psychology and motivation. The outcome was that between 1995 and 1997 North-Rhine-Westphalia recorded a 6 per cent increase in the foundation of new businesses, compared with a mere 0.6 per cent in the rest of the country. Between 1997 and 1998 about a quarter of a million people set up on their own. Even measured against insolvencies and businesses that closed down for other reasons, the balance remained positive.

Because, for a variety of reasons, a considerable number of new businesses would fail after five years without assistance, 'Go!' sends in 'coaches' – experienced ex-managers, for instance – to give advice. This has proved a highly successful initiative. An employer setting up an apprenticeship training scheme would receive a one-off grant of 20,000 marks. If one assumes that after a few years each such successful business produces between three and five new jobs – a generally accepted figure – each new job costs on average 6,000 marks. In West Germany as a whole the ratio of employers setting up new businesses, which had fallen in the 1980s to less than 7 per cent, also rose, to almost 10 per cent. In 1997, 530,000 new businesses opened and 440,000 folded. In order to stem these losses concrete help is needed, together with the creation of an atmosphere more conducive to the establishment of new companies. The universities, for example, could have a role to play in this. There have been a few isolated attempts to create university posts for the purpose of teaching students about how to go about setting up in business for themselves, but, all in all, few graduates show much interest. One of the most important areas would be the co-operation between science and industry.

Recent years have also brought changes in Germany's attitude towards the provision of risk capital. On the initiative of the provincial government of North-Rhine-Westphalia, a fund has been set up to make venture capital available. The *Land* underwrites this fund and guarantees up to 90 per cent of the equity in each individual case.

But there remains a gap in providing for someone who does not want to set up in some area of the high-tech market but only needs a few thousand marks in order, for example, to open a shop. The programmes put forward in North-Rhine-Westphalia reflect an awareness that we need a fundamentally new culture of capital provision. This involves, on the one hand, our local banks and their credit policies, on the other hand, the tax treatment of venture capital. The unequal tax treatment of such capital compared with other forms of investment leaves Germany languishing well behind other industrialized nations. One cannot, of course, compare Germany with the USA but even in the UK the volume of venture capital is more than four times that in Germany. We must make it profitable again to invest in factories and jobs, not in empty buildings.

The importance for the labour market of a readiness to set up in business for oneself – and of an official policy to support such initiatives – is emphasized by the problems that arise when such businesses change hands. In the near future, in North-Rhine-Westphalia alone, almost 80,000 middle-ranking employers and tradespeople will be retiring from their own firms for reasons of age, and the transfer from one generation to the next will accelerate in the years ahead. There would be nothing worrying about this, were it not for the fact that for 20,000 of these employers there is as yet no successor. If we assume, conservatively, that each of these businesses employs an average of ten employees, then at least 200,000 jobs are at risk. In manual trades there are even surveys that show that only one-third of such businesses will survive into the next generation; the other two-thirds will simply disappear. The same situation applies to all the other *Länder*. In North-Rhine-Westphalia, starting in specially chosen areas, potential founders of new businesses are being put into contact with employers who are looking for a successor.

All this shows how important it is to make the running of an independent business a serious prospect for many more people today. Such examples should be made a model for others to copy. 'The obligation to promote independence, in the broadest sense, in a free society cannot be confined to individual groups.' This was said as long ago as 1960 by Müller-Armack, Ludwig Erhard's comrade-in-arms. Erhard himself sensed in the mid-1950s that the concept of the state as provider would progressively erode the spirit of adventure, ambition, personal initiative and a sense of communal responsibility. We would be well advised not to allow the most important precondition for all social and economic modernization to reach the point where the state has to prove that it can do itself, as well or even better, what it demands from others. The state must never permit itself to believe that it can be the best of all employers.

Despite the gloomy forecasts about an uneconomic state, and despite accusations of corruption in government, one must make it quite clear that central and local government in Germany is still one of the most reliable in the world – though this does not mean, of course, that there are not areas of incompetence and inefficiency which must be got rid of.

Perhaps the most serious criticism that can be levelled at officialdom is that it has become too passive, too concerned with red tape, whereas it should adopt a proactive role. We also need to examine the criticism that the state is not flexible enough, is not sufficiently concerned with the needs of the citizen, is not cost-conscious and works too slowly. The much-publicized deficits usually lead to a demand for the privatization of public expenditure. But a more efficient bureaucracy cannot be achieved by threats. A large proportion of the problems that smaller companies, in particular, have with the authorities are purely matters of communication. The man in the street speaks a different language from the bureaucrat and each has difficulties in dealing with the other. The proactive state is no longer just a provider that makes its services available for nothing. Its guiding principles are transparency, efficiency and honesty in those areas for which it retains responsibility. It needs to become more efficient in all fields and to put this efficiency at the disposal of private citizens and the business community.

An individual who has any dealings with state agencies must be helped to develop initiatives, make investments, show commitment and assume responsibilities. Any move to modernize the economy must not stop at the door of the state. Bureaucratic procedures that have been in place for almost 180 years are no longer capable of dealing with structural change. Many bodies, particularly local authorities, have shed large numbers of jobs over recent years so as to meet their responsibility to produce a balanced budget, but in some cases the economies have gone too far. A number of towns have found that, for instance, by appointing additional employees with an expertise in job placement, social security offices can save millions of marks a year. This shows dramatically that the model of the 'slimmed-down state' must not be carried too far.

Instead, we must lay out afresh what the duties and functions of the state are, and subject these duties and functions to radical re-examination. In a recent survey conducted in Lower Saxony people were asked what functions could equally well, or even better, be carried out by private organizations – with the same guarantees, of course, as those required of the state. While school education, internal security and the legal framework were held to be the fundamental province of the state, a considerable number of people were in favour of handing over responsibility for such things as street-cleaning, refuse-collection, the construction and maintenance of roads and the provision of adult education to private organizations. Over a third of those polled were of the opinion that kindergartens could be more efficiently run by the public themselves.

It would also doubtless be applauded if we were to tackle the long-overdue problem of debureaucratization. We must set about revising, simplifying or, in the last analysis, repealing at least

2,000 federal laws and 3,000 statutes – a total of more than 85,000 clauses! Licensing authorities should not be obstructive. In the Netherlands certain laws have a limited life-span – so-called 'sunset legislation' – and are constantly checked for their efficacy. In Germany the *Land* of Lower Saxony has made a start on a similar programme to review the effects of legislation. 'Don't let documents collect dust' is the motto. Any attempt to modernize society entails modernizing the state as well.

During the Kohl era, in which the ideals of deregulation and privatization were held high, the bureaucratic burden on small and medium-sized business almost doubled. Today, the federal government has ratified 1,400 laws, ordinances and procedural measures in the field of environment law alone. Building laws have proliferated. From 1982 to 1998 the conservative government passed 1,518 new laws, 1,064 of them on the basis of government bills. For every rule abolished, ten new ones sprang up.

The best example for demonstrating that efficiency must be made the acid test of the activities of the state is that of the transport system. The question of road versus rail was always a sterile argument. Equally pointless was the idea that by restricting road construction, especially the autobahn network, people could be made to switch to public transport. We must not treat one means of transport as superior to all the others: each has its place, the area in which it works to its maximum efficiency. The entire transport infrastructure must be comprehensively planned and greater use made of electronic facilities such as the so-called Personal Travel Assistant – a gadget little bigger than a mobile phone that can tell the user at all times and all places the distance of his or her destination, how long the journey will take, which is the most suitable means of transport to choose and so on.

Transportation is by far the largest receiver of state subsidies in Germany – almost 45 billion marks a year. Total capacity can hardly be increased, therefore we must seek all possible ways and means of operating more efficiently. Take the car. Traffic jams are harmful to the environment, since fuel is wasted and exhaust gases produced that benefit no one. The ADAC, the German motorists' organization, puts the total cost of traffic jams on German roads at 200 billion marks a year. Such a figure can only be a rough estimate. But such uneconomic conditions, accidents, wasted energy and avoidable exhaust emissions are all unacceptable. The financing of new autobahns is virtually beyond our means, therefore we must extend those that we have and make them more efficient. Experts have long since produced evidence on how jams can be avoided. One is to move from road to rail. The railways have recently become more competitive in respect of the movement of freight, and the opportunity to transfer from road to rail is a real one. But one has to make an effort. In industrial areas like the Ruhr, for example, disused rail track left by derelict industries could be put to practical use.

Automobiles, and especially heavy goods vehicles, endanger the environment. Everyone knows that we are paying a heavy price, in safety and many other fields, for our personal mobility and for the freight traffic that chokes our roads. I have no wish to join the debate on the alleged or actual external costs of motoring – it is a debate that has done little to advance the arguments over transport policy. What would help, however, would be an improvement in the comfort, safety and frequency of public transport, so that drivers would be tempted out of their cars.

As to freight traffic, the privileged position of road traffic must be reversed. Concrete steps are needed to change the distorted competitive system which penalizes rail and waterway traffic, and to transfer motorized traffic to environment-friendlier means of transport – to train and bus, as far as the travelling public is concerned, and to rail and water for freight traffic. Demands for people to restrict their journeys are completely unrealistic. If one wishes to minimize the pollution that cars undoubtedly cause, one must create the conditions in which better cars can be built – cars that consume less energy, produce less toxic emissions, are quieter and above all safer.

We have made considerable progress in these areas in recent years. By the year 2005, taking 1987–8 as the point of departure, emissions in respect of nitrous oxides will be reduced by 32 per cent, hydrocarbons by 69 per cent and benzol by 66 per cent, in spite of a rising volume of traffic on the roads and improvements in automobile performance. This is due in the first instance to the use of catalytic converters. Diesel engines demand our special attention, and here too technical advances will help to reduce the problems.

Fuel consumption poses very special difficulties. In recent years the average fuel consumption of all cars in Germany has fallen by some 12 per cent, but part of the potential gain was offset by an increase in vehicle weight and the trend towards bigger engines.

I have described the situation in such detail because I am of the opinion that, in terms of energy policy and environment policy, a three-litre car can only be acceptable if it can be introduced into the market on a massive scale. Many people have yet to be convinced of this. New fuels and technologies, such as electric and solar-powered vehicles, will only be crowned with success if we press ahead with technological development and with preparing the market, while at the same time making the social climate more conducive to accepting these developments. Another reason why we must aim at finding technological solutions to environmental problems is that we cannot prescribe for the people living in countries whose prosperity is based on the forces of globalization what degree of mobility they shall enjoy. The mobility that we have created for ourselves – what we call freedom of movement – is something they also wish for. The increase in traffic in countries that are today part of the Third World will release an unprecedented demand for energy. It would be helpful if Germany could invent a mobility technology that could help to keep the energy and environmental consequences of this explosion within bounds and make mobility financially sustainable.

If we look at the question in terms of the needs of society, it is clear that we do not have too much technology but too little. What is happening in the field of transport is also happening in many other fields. Taking steps to avoid wastefulness, remove blockages in bureaucratic procedures and minimize friction serves economic, environmental and social purposes at one and the same time. Such blockages are not just minor irritations in the market economy but absorb a large part of the available resources. If one adds together the cost of crime and crime prevention, the cost of the destruction of the environment and wasted natural resources, the annual figure of some 300 billion dollars to meet the cost of unemployment in the industrialized nations, and the cost of the damage to health – then one arrives at a figure of 10,000 billion dollars a year, which is five times German domestic product and a third of the domestic product of the entire world.

Even if these figures may be speculative to some extent, one is still left with the fact, for example, that faulty diets cost 100 billion marks a year in Germany. Around 50 per cent of research and development expenditure is swallowed up by information deficits in patent offices, while experts put the cost of traffic jams at 200 billion marks a year. The efficiency reserves in the health system which could be achieved without any redundancies amount to 25 billion marks. Even the psychological consequences of bullying – a growing feature of life in factories and offices – have been said to cost 30 billion marks every year. All this shows that there is a huge market for innovation and change in society.

New industries could be developed and competitiveness as a whole considerably improved in all manner of areas – nature conservation, health, biotechnology and trade are among the most important. In the public health sector alone it has been calculated that productivity could be increased by 30 per cent without the need for redundancies. The USA has followed the same path, with a remarkable effect on the employment situation. Greater efficiency throughout the country and better-crafted political programmes will put us in a position to solve our problems in the areas of employment and social security.

In North-Rhine-Westphalia we have made a start in this direction on the basis of a co-operative economic policy. In co-operation with the captains of industry, we shall examine who is best suited to deal with individual questions, how one side can help the other and how duplication – and unproductive rivalry – can be avoided. The old notion of subsidiarity is acquiring a new relevance, as recently demonstrated in the field of overseas trade. Chambers of commerce, foreign branches of large concerns, state advisory bodies, organizers of trade fairs – all are brought together under one roof. And new subjects are constantly being discovered which lend themselves to discussion in these co-operative terms.

7

Policies for a Proactive Society

The greatest political scandal in Germany today is mass unemployment. The official figure stands at 4.8 million, to which must be added at least a further 2 million in concealed unemployment, in training and work programmes or those who have simply withdrawn from the labour market altogether. In the country as a whole there are around 7 million unfilled vacancies.

Three-quarters of our unemployment has structural causes. For over 25 years economic recovery has always followed from an ever-growing basic core of unemployed. From 1970 unemployment in the former West Germany rose after each successive recession by at least 700,000, and even in phases of strong economic recovery the proportion never fell by more than 1–2.5 per cent. At the end of the 1970s the government and both sides of industry declared the fight against unemployment to be their prime concern, but words were not followed by deeds.

In comparative international analyses long-term unemployment is always taken as the yardstick for measuring the innovative power of the economy, the mobility of the workforce, the flexibility of wages and hours of work, the regulation of the labour market, the employment effects of social security and the efficiency of training programmes. Against the background of the prevailing conditions in the labour market, and given the traditional features of employment policy in Germany, a growing number of unemployed are no longer employable. In 1998 one-third of the

4.8 million unemployed had been without a job for a year or longer. For millions of others a spell of unemployment was regarded as virtually inevitable. On a given day in 1996 826,000 were registered as unemployed in North-Rhine-Westphalia, but the number of people looking for work, whether for the first time or on repeated occasions, amounted in that year to 1.3 million. For more and more people unemployment is becoming neither a permanent state of affairs nor a separate, short-lived period but a constantly recurring condition, alternating with periods of work.

We are running the risk of having the 'losers' lagging further and further behind the 'winners'. This has devastating effects when it comes to youth unemployment. For the first time in ten years more young adults were unemployed in 1997 than corresponded to their proportion of the total number of those in work and paying social security contributions. Of unemployed youths under the age of 20, 90 per cent have no professional qualification, and for the man or woman who has no access to a 'second chance' via the dual system it is really the end of the road. Qualities such as team spirit, loyalty, reliability, punctuality and dealings with one's superiors are things learnt and practised on the job, but a person denied access to these things finds it more and more difficult to get into employment, and all attempts to do so become more and more frustrating. An enquiry commissioned by the government of North-Rhine-Westphalia under the heading 'The Future of Gainful Employment' issued a warning that this frustration can lead to gang warfare, criminal behaviour and political radicalism, especially in the large cities.

On the other hand, the long-term unemployed do not necessarily form a marginalized group that is permanently ostracized from society or is in particular need of care. Many social workers take this view, but it does not square with the facts. The young unemployed person usually wants only one thing – to be spared a visit from a social worker and to find a job again as quickly as possible.

One fact is striking. In North-Rhine-Westphalia the proportion of long-term unemployed between the ages of 20 and 44 has been falling since 1994, whereas the proportion of unemployed over-45s has been rising over the same period. There is a tendency on the part of young people to take short-term employment or find part-time jobs or casual work of some kind – jobs, in other words, that offer little challenge and carry no security. Without such opportunities, however, even more young people would feel abandoned.

In North-Rhine-Westphalia, between 1990 and 1996, 1.5 million jobs a year – i.e. one in four of all those in regular employment – were either started or given up. This had serious consequences for the labour market, which had not yet adjusted to such flexibility. There is a need for accompanying measures to assist in getting people quickly back into work. The decisive consideration for unemployed individuals is whether or not the interruption in their employment is only temporary, in which case they would have a chance to gain a further qualification. This depends, however, on the flexibility of the labour market and the nature of the government's employment policy. If we cling to our ideal of standard, full-time employment, we shall soon find ourselves facing standard, full-time *un*employment.

Yet for years we have all seen this crisis coming. By the middle of the 1980s it had become obvious that the pressure being put on industry to raise productivity would lead to job losses and interruptions in work patterns, together with changes in the nature of the skills required. In neighbouring Holland they began to put into practice some of the new ideas – redistribution of jobs, for example – that had been on the table for some time. In Germany, however, we got bogged down in arid debates that led nowhere. People talked of 'a national crisis', and journalists wrote about 'the end of work'. To cap it all, Chancellor Kohl pledged to halve unemployment by the year 2000.

Let us be clear on one thing – it is an illusion to believe that our society is going to run out of work. Other countries have created new jobs and reallocated old ones – and that in the face of globalization. The amount of work in a national economy is not like a cake that can be cut up in different ways but only eaten once. We are constantly producing new jobs and fields of activity, while old jobs disappear. At the present time there are not enough jobs in the service sectors to compensate for the losses in industry. Whereas in America the job threshold stands at 0.6 per cent of growth, in Germany the figure is put at 2.5 per cent. That is to say, we need growth of this order of magnitude in order to generate one new job. So we find ourselves facing the question: why cannot the two million companies and administrative authorities in Germany produce enough jobs for all?

Among the economic answers given are too slow a rate of innovation, problems of orientation in the service industries, discrepancies between the skills required and the qualifications the training schemes turn out. A precondition for a permanent change in the employment situation is dynamic growth. But one problem that cannot be solved by growth alone is so-called 'mismatch' unemployment. New jobs do not become vacant at the same time, in the same place or requiring the same qualifications, as those which have just been lost. While low-skill industrial workers give up hope, machine-tool factories are crying out for engineers. In the case of academic qualifications and skilled workers it depends on the flexibility and initiative of the applicant whether or not new job opportunities can be taken up. Take telecommunications, for instance. The principal factor restricting its growth is the shortage of highly qualified experts. The multi-media industry had 75,000 unfilled positions in 1998, and a further 14,000 were not created because the interest of school-leavers in courses in information sciences and engineering had declined in recent years to a point where there were simply not enough qualified people available. The thousands of vacant apprenticeships in a variety of trades which cannot be filled, in spite of an alleged 'crisis' in the availability of apprenticeships, are a further symptom of a divided labour market and too little flexibility. There is work to be had, but nobody is there to do it.

In the summer of 1997 the Hamburg Chamber of Commerce published figures to show that the city had 93,500 registered unemployed, as against some 100,000 in the 'black' economy. Economists assess the proportion of illegal work as between 10 and 15 per cent of gross domestic product, with an upwards tendency. According to government figures, this means that the state is thereby losing 50 billion marks a year in taxes and social security contributions. But as long as a worker has to put in three or more hours in order to be able to afford a single one of his own working hours – as long, that is, as the gap between gross and net remains as wide as it is – many new jobs will never find their way on to the regular labour market but will stay outside it. If one accepts the broadest definition of this fraudulent self-employment, one arrives at a total figure of almost 700,000 workers who earn a living for themselves and their families, are dependent on an employer but never figure in the employment statistics.

The Hamburg Chamber of Commerce concluded:

It is not that we have too little work. The fact is that, owing to high taxation, employers' added costs and bureaucratic regulations, a considerable proportion of the work available is no longer affordable. The same reasons are also responsible for the further fact that not every person registered as unemployed is necessarily looking for a job in the 'official' market.

What is being totally destroyed by this radical development is the concept of normality that underlies the exercise of our entire social and employment policy. We are experiencing a creeping de-institutionalization that is changing the nature of the labour market, making a mockery of our traditional notions of lifelong, full-time employment and undermining the foundations of our social security. There is no easy way of stopping this. If we cannot learn to introduce flexible practices into the pattern of people's working lives, and promote further training and refresher courses, continuing to look askance at part-time and short-term jobs and make them unattractive by withholding adequate social security measures, then we shall only accelerate the trend.

Our policies continue to cling to the old 'normal' conception of work, foundation of a static model of life with permanent employment and guaranteed social security provision, enjoying all legal and negotiated rights, with fixed hours of work, protected against possible loss of income through insurance arrangements, and with a guaranteed pension at the end of one's working days. Germany has always had difficulties with concepts of 'irregular' employment. It took an unconscionable time before the SPD was prepared to admit that workers must be ready to work in two or three different fields in the course of their working lives. But events overtook us. Over the country as a whole 83.4 per cent of the workforce were still in permanent full-time jobs in 1970. By 1996 the figure had fallen to 66.7 per cent.

Today all parties accept that part-time working forms part of the strategy for the redistribution of the available work. An institute working on behalf of the Federal Ministry of Labour found that of the 5.5 million increase of those in employment recorded since 1960, 4 million, i.e. almost three-quarters, were in part-time employment. Yet compared with other countries, Germany is still way behind in this field. We need a broad flexibilization in working hours which also includes the public sector.

A linear reduction in working hours for men and women to thirty-two or even thirty hours per week, as proposed in 1997 by Klaus Zwickel, president of the IG-Metall union, can only be an average figure; the actual number of hours worked will fluctuate according to individual situation, economic circumstances and the needs of production. A reduction in working hours must be accompanied by flexi-time working. One pattern could be that recently introduced by Volkswagen, whereby variable hours of work can be 'stored', as in a bank account, credit being given for hours worked. At the same time flexible individual plans should be co-ordinated with the need for periods of further training – an analogy to the periodical 'sabbaticals' taken by university lecturers and professors. There can be no single, unified pattern. What is required from all parties – employees, unions and employers, and not least in the policies of the government – is a spirit of creativity and imagination.

In contrast, however, to the growing consensus over working times, our approach to what are obstinately called 'irregular' forms of employment is characteristic of our attitude towards the short-comings of the welfare system – the attitude that reality has to adapt itself to our welfare system, not vice versa. The flexibilization schemes created by the labour market, especially at its bottom end, serve rather to put people off than to be seen as offering them a fresh opportunity. The left wing has no idea how those on welfare who have never been integrated into the labour market can be freed from their dependency on the state. The question is whether more flexible forms of employment could not also act as a buffer, rather than be seen as only whittling away the amount of the work available. Many regard them as a preference rather than as a compulsion.

In the Netherlands every second newly created job is with a company that has adopted temporary working. In the USA more than 34 million are working on short-term contracts, and between 1982 and 1990 the number of temporary workers rose ten times as fast as the total number in employment. In Germany, too, though to a large extent unnoticed, the number of legally employed temporary workers has grown enormously. The number of firms permitted to employ workers on temporary loan has risen by a factor of three to a total of 9,000 and the proportion of workers on temporary loan has risen over tenfold, reaching a figure of almost 200,000 by 1998.

A third of loan workers stay less than a year in that category, while an appreciable proportion are taken over into full-time or permanent part-time employment. The contribution made by temporary workers to solving the general problem of unemployment should not be ignored. According to an analysis by the Institute for Industry and Society in Bonn, about half of temporary workers belong to one or other of the so-called 'problem groups' – foreigners, those over 45 years of age, unskilled or low-skilled workers, those who had previously been unemployed or had given up employment for some while – to raise a family, for example. Many come from industries that have been laying off large numbers of workers in recent years. For instance, 40 per cent came from the electrical and metalworking industries. Attempts to reintegrate them met with no success, but without this interim measure two-thirds of them would be unemployed, and for them temporary work is the best way to a new job and the retention of their qualifications. Even the trade-union organization for the *Land* of North-Rhine-Westphalia, after years of resistance, has finally come round to the idea that temporary work is an acceptable part of employment policy.

Since the beginning of 1995 North-Rhine-Westphalia, in co-operation with the trade unions, employers' organizations and other bodies, has been working on a regional programme called START, aimed at evolving a model for the reintegration of unemployed workers into a working environment. In thirty-three regional offices attempts are being made to offer, ultimately, permanent employment to the hard-core unemployed by means of temporary spells of work in factories. To date, 6,000 have taken part in the scheme and every second worker subsequently found a permanent job. It is calculated that by the year 2003 this market will have trebled. Two out of three came from specially targeted areas of the labour market, and almost a third had been long-term unemployed. Financed from public funds, including subsidies from the European Union, the scheme provides workers with 'certificates of competence', sets agreed rates of pay, gives them a qualification and submits to inspections by unions and management.

The highlight of the START scheme is its degressive funding. In 1998 the participating firms even made a profit. In the first year of its operation the scheme showed a surplus of 3.5 million marks.

A similar success seems likely to follow the scheme introduced into so-called 'welfare support' firms in North-Rhine-Westphalia, Lower Saxony and elsewhere. Here, firms that have undertaken to employ a large proportion of long-term unemployed are heavily subsidized for a number of years until they have found a market for their products and can stand on their own feet. As these markets are usually in goods not already being produced in the area in question – the repair and sale of second-hand furniture or textiles, for instance – the scheme also has a beneficial effect on the local economy.

In order to combine flexi-time working with further training, a start has been made on a scheme of 'job rotation', which draws on experience gathered in Denmark. A worker leaves his job, which is held open for him, for a maximum of 24 months, in order to study for a further qualification which his employer requires of him. The nature of the qualification is discussed between the parties. The worker's security is guaranteed by a state-funded further training allowance of 75 per cent of his last net pay, refinanced by savings in unemployment allowance and other state payments. The employer then makes up the total sum to 90 per cent of the worker's last net pay. The cost of the training scheme itself is borne by the state. The social security of the unemployed worker who returns to take up his job is met by a wage payment from the employer amounting to 90 per cent of the standard wage applicable to the work performed.

For employers and for the state the model is to a large degree cost-neutral. The regulations should be drawn up on the basis of existing wage agreements or legally binding individual contracts. The acceptance of the model would release more than 200,000 jobs per year. In the Netherlands the proportion of those working in part-time jobs because they are at the same time engaged on a further training course is high – almost one-third of males in part-time employment are taking advantage of this flexibility to prepare themselves for a more highly qualified job.

There is thus no shortage of schemes for dealing with the situation. Maybe we shall eventually come to see part-time work, temporary jobs, casual employment and even state-sponsored jobs as normal aspects of the market. But the argument in 1997 over low-paid jobs made it painfully clear what problems we still have with a labour market that can no longer be forced into a rigid framework.

Not a few of the problem groups have found in recent years that a low-paid job has opened up new prospects for them. Such jobs may not be ideal but they do offer fresh opportunities – simple jobs in the service industries, jobs for low-skill workers or for those who for one reason or another are unable to hold down a full-time position. Two-thirds of workers only want, or are only able, to work a few hours a week, maybe because they are following a course of training or because they have children to look after. It is not without reason that 40 per cent of such jobs are done by women between the ages of 25 and 44. In the face of the growing number of single mothers – the figure rose from 1.27 million in 1991 to 1.52 million in 1997 – it is a scandal that jobs for people in this position can hardly be found.

Jobs exempt from social security contributions cannot be considered an unmitigated success in political terms, not least because, as the only exemption from compulsory national insurance, they are indirectly subsidized by the state. We must avoid splitting regular full-time jobs into a number of part-time jobs. At the same time it would be a retrograde step to extend the rigidity of the 'normal' job structure into those sectors of the market where casual jobs have a role to play. What we must ensure is that both the inducements and the disadvantages, financial and social, are brought into play where they are needed and removed where they are not. We need a system of welfare contributions which is fair and acceptable to worker and employer alike and which keeps down administrative costs, thereby relieving the pressure on the system as a whole.

One thing is clear. All attempts to exploit the advantages of flexibilization at the lower end of the labour market will be in vain unless we succeed in detaching the social security systems from the assumption of a 'normal', lifetime, full-time job and a 'normal' family, with the father as the breadwinner, providing for his wife and children. The most effective way of preventing the spread of low-paid jobs is to remove the burden of employers' compulsory added costs. And 'irregular' jobs as a means of access to the labour market will only be successful if it is made genuinely attractive for a person on welfare to take up supplementary work, instead of finding that each additional mark he or she earns is confiscated by the state. As our policy must be to help businesses exposed to international competition to retain their competitive position through innovative practices, so reforms to the welfare system must ensure that low-skill workers are offered new opportunities of employment.

Defining Crisis in a Welfare State

Today we are paying the price for the inability of the welfare state to conceive of solidarity and unity other than in terms of costs and statistics. The single-minded philosophy that more welfare benefits means greater fairness has come back to haunt us, because the system has taken on such dimensions that common-or-garden wage-earners can hardly grasp the meaning of their pay-slips. In 1997 Germany spent 1,256 billion marks on welfare benefits, 20 per cent more than the preceding year, and it is forecast that this figure will rise to 1,345 billion by the year 2001, i.e. an annual increase of 1.7 per cent. The lion's share of this will be borne, as before, by employers and employees – 65.8 per cent by 2001.

Today all the well-established principles of social security, hitherto accepted by all the parties concerned as a reasonable basis for agreement, are being put under the microscope, but nobody is bringing the various reform proposals together in a single context. There is a sense of helplessness because nowhere can a paradigm be found which could form the foundation of a new consensus over the shape that the social security system of tomorrow should take.

The sociologist Claus Offe distinguished three types of crisis in the welfare state, which he illustrated with an anecdote. Imagine, he said, that a dam has burst (an appropriate image in the face of the rising tide of welfare contributions). Three men see the situation from three different angles. The first has his house swept away in the flood and claims on his insurance; the second is a structural engineer commissioned by the insurance company; and the third is an environmentalist who was opposed to building the dam in the first place. The houseowner will be glad if the event can be put down to natural forces or an act of God, because in that case the insurance company will pay out. The engineer will suspect that it was due to faulty materials or bad design, while the environmentalist will look for ecological causes, maintaining, for example, that the locality was unsuitable for a dam in the first place. In consequence, the houseowner will want to increase his insurance premiums, the engineer will call for technical changes in construction, and the environmentalist will invoke wider ecological arguments.

It is a strikingly apt analogy. External causes – the demographic situation and its effect on the labour market, changes in household and family patterns, German reunification, European economic and currency union, globalization – seem to many, like our houseowner, to be forces of nature which one cannot do other than accept. He therefore insists on compensation from his insurance company, which, in turn, faced with rising claims, raises its premiums and reduces its pay-outs.

But anybody who has listened to the debates that have been taking place over the last fifteen years will put the blame on the intrinsic features of the system. Because the social security system is based on the concept of gainful employment in the form of long-term, full-time employment, and in its financial aspects depends entirely on the number of those thus employed, mass unemployment and new modes of work lead to a vicious circle of increased benefits, diminishing funds and over-priced labour. The sheer pressure causes the dam to give way.

The situation is aggravated by the fact that the welfare state does not guarantee a defined subsistence level and a chance for the individual to make a fresh start but only a certain status and a certain standard of living. In guaranteeing above all the rights of those who have faithfully paid their social security contributions, the state provides both too much and too little welfare. This is apparently regarded as rational because it ensures the political support of the main political bodies. At the same time, in the face of the growing lack of public confidence, one wonders whether the population would not willingly give up this 'hush-money' if they could only be offered new and reliable guarantees, especially as the individual's opportunities to influence his outlay and his projected benefits are steadily declining. In his book *A New Age* (1996) Gerd Dahlmanns wrote:

The individual is never asked about such matters, even though his vital interests are at stake. It is politicians who make the decisions about percentage points in these systems. It is the organizations to which he is forced to belong that take his money and decide how much he will get in return. The result is an absurd, backward-looking type of welfare state which withholds from the man caught up in it two vital pieces of information – what costs he entails by claiming particular benefits, and what he actually earns in his job.

Up to now the state has guaranteed security by means of welfare entitlements and payments. But in so doing, it left open the question 'How much is enough?' This was a standing invitation to organizations of all kinds, the parties and assorted pressure groups to interpret and extend welfare claims to suit their own interests, and embark on a 'competitive insurance spiral'. The conservatives' criticism of the way costs were escalating and of the development of cliques and coteries within the system is not easy to dismiss.

The debate on the abuse of benefits conceals the fact that the benefits and costs spiral results, not from abuse in the legal sense but from perfectly legal claims made in conformity with the regulations. Economic necessity does not stop at the door of a person on welfare. Economists talk of a 'poverty trap' created by the state, whereby many find it preferable to accept a welfare cheque than to take a poorly paid job. Others are driven by the high insurance deductions to look for moonlighting jobs. The standard contribution rate for social security, half paid by the employer, half by the employee, is higher than ever. Forecasts that this would happen were dismissed as scaremongering.

Recent studies show that in its present form the benefits system serves rather to extend than reduce the period of unemployment. A man becomes classified as showing 'little inclination to work'. The Institute for Employment and Technology in Gelsenkirchen puts the proportion of those who, for reasons of age or disinclination to work, have left the workforce once and for all at a quarter of all long-term unemployed. Many unemployment projects and state-funded initiatives perpetuate the frustration caused by unemployment rather than alleviate it. We have seen from our experience in East Germany how quickly unemployment schemes that are not integrated into the regional economic structure and made part of economic policy only serve to foster a mentality of dependency on subsidies.

Maybe this is putting things too bluntly. But as things stand, welfare system and employment policy tend to make the unemployed feel – for as long as they draw unemployment money – as though they have had an accident, or – from the time they are reduced to basic welfare – that they have become a victim of the ruthlessness of the market.

In his book *Will Germany Fail?* (1997), Arnulf Baring wrote:

In the eyes of many people, including politicians, 'reasonable' is a relative term. It may be 'reasonable' for an untrained, under-privileged man to take on dirty, unpleasant work, but not for an academic or a member of the middle classes.

But is there such menial work in Germany today? Millions of Germans dig their gardens over every year, lay turf and decorate their houses, collecting blisters and bruises on the way. Classless labour unites the millionaire and the allotment-holder, the Nobel prizewinner and the shop assistant who decorates her room at the weekend. How can such jobs be 'unreasonable' for one who has the misfortune to be dependent on the state?

Many sociologists see such work undergoing a magic trans-formation – from being a source of individual self-fulfilment to one person it becomes a degrading way of earning a living to another. This is certainly to overstate the point. But when a new shopping and leisure centre opened in the centre of the town of Oberhausen in 1996, and new sales assistants had to be recruited, 40 per cent of the applicants failed one simple test. A manager pretending to be a customer entered the store and either asked for assistance or made a complaint. Some of the applicants shrugged their shoulders, others became aggressive. So much for courtesy being 'reasonable'.

Politicians are under an obligation to strike a new balance between guaranteed rights and proactive obligations. They must be clear about the areas in which they should, and can, inter-vene. Over recent decades politics has intruded more and more deeply into every aspect of our daily lives, with the result that we have been given promises that could not be kept and an arrogant assumption of authority which could only end in disillusionment.

In his book *The Politics of Society* (1997) the sociologist Niklas Luhmann wrote:

When it is a matter of deciding one way or the other, it is always the political system that is held responsible for compensating people for damage caused by acts of fate. Failed harvests are as much a drain on public funds as giving birth or having an abortion. Sufferers from obesity seek help, so do the victims of accidents, run-down industries and expensive technological failures. The dramatic rise in the number of physicists leads to an even more dramatic rise in research grants, while progress in medicine has the double effect of increasing the costs both of treatment and research.

All this is perfectly justifiable, or at least fully legitimate in its own terms. Demands that stem from this are neither absurd nor defamatory – they are built into the political system as a means of political communication. In the end the state is like a water tower in which funds are first pumped up, then distributed to anyone who is connected to the supply.

From Safety Net to Trampoline

To introduce cuts only in areas of least resistance is to ask for trouble. There is only one way for the welfare state to set about making savings in its operations, namely by subjecting every programme and every institution to the acid test – do we really get for our money what we expected? We need a new, positive conception of the welfare state, for the success of a welfare state cannot be measured by the amounts of money it pays out. There is not even an unambiguous empirical relationship between the welfare budget and the success of our employment policies. The old division by which the left hand collects more money which it then redistributes through the tax system, while the right hand reduces taxation and saves money, has become irrelevant.

The catchword of left-wing politics is fairness, i.e. social justice – justice for those who need assistance but also for those who pay for it. In 1997 alone unemployment cost the country 180 billion marks – loss of tax revenue and insurance contributions, increased welfare payments and the assumption by the state of responsibility for insurance contributions. This money should be invested in work, not in unemployment. We must plan a modernization of the mechanisms by which the state seeks to create equality of opportunity. We need a labour market which may not guarantee a job for life but which facilitates diversification and movement in and out of jobs. The objective is no longer to have periods of unemployment but only periods of adjustment, of retraining and requalifying, or of domestic and honorary work. Under the conservative government the idea had become firmly established that provision for unemployment was so comprehensive that one could easily get used to the idea of not having a job as a normal state of affairs for one part of the population.

A comparison with other countries clearly demonstrates that states which succeed in modernizing their instruments have done so by taking the best features of a variety of models and combining them into one. In a time of change, to adhere to the status quo gives the individual not more security but less. Employment policies must say goodbye to the standard full-time job as the absolute point of reference, and an employment and qualifications policy can no longer function without the participation of individual companies. We must convert our labour administration into a 'jobs service' which encourages diversification and mobility.

The financial crisis facing the redistributive state offers the proactive welfare state its great opportunity. Why should it be considered socially more responsible to take people's responsibility away than to help them to assume responsibility for themselves? People are wiser than we think. They know that we have been living beyond our means and that our welfare system is prone to develop in the wrong direction. Suggestions from local politicians would be accepted if people could see the point of them – 'The public must share in the work of keeping the swimming-pools and playgrounds clean. Your council cannot do the work by itself. Without your help we shall be forced to close the libraries' – and so on. In Canada taxpayers are sent a letter by the local tax office laying out in detail what proportion of their tax is spent on what services. Road repair signs in the USA do not say, as in Germany, 'Warning! Delays!', but 'Your Tax Dollar Is Working Here'.

If a welfare state redistributes monies rather than opportunities, it is heading for a fall. We must ask of every institution whether it promotes and rewards individual responsibility and individual initiative or whether it induces passivity and resignation. We could illustrate the difference through the image of the safety net and the trampoline. On the one side the much-criticized protection of the state hammock, ready to catch anyone who falls; on the other side the trampoline, which not only saves anyone from falling but bounces him back into a life of work, of responsibility and self-confidence, of reintegration into society.

State intervention is only legitimate when it promotes and challenges the individual's abilities and sense of initiative, and does not just guarantee his material well-being. This is the proper meaning of the principle of subsidiarity – not a way of economizing by the individualization of risk, or a way of shrugging off one's responsibility on to the state, but a proactive concept which brings with it the possibility of a second chance.

North-Rhine-Westphalia has embarked on a new initiative to tackle the problem of long-term youth unemployment. Working in co-operation with employers, long-term unemployed youths are offered a job in a company for a year. In return they commit themselves to attend a course of training which will provide a qualification. A scheme of this kind is already in force in Denmark, while other European countries too are revising their traditional conceptions of employment and making radical changes in their systems. In the Netherlands, Sweden, the UK and other countries the motto is now 'Any job is better than none'. With a handful of exceptions, no jobs are regarded as inferior. I am convinced that any work, however poorly qualified and poorly paid, serves the cause of human dignity and self-esteem better than the most generous of welfare benefits. And, of course, willingness to accept a job under these terms must be matched by a promise from the state that the work done will be properly paid for and leave a fair sum in the worker's pocket.

Whereas the marginal utility of German employment policy is steadily falling, the Netherlands, for example, succeeds in placing at least as many people in regular work for a considerably smaller outlay in wage subsidies. They have managed both to liberalize the labour market and retain welfare provisions, and, thanks to a combination of flexible working and a proactive employment policy, they have achieved substantially greater flexibility at the lower end of the market than Germany. We can also learn from the way the Dutch have modernized their administrative procedures and from their success with those who had no prospect of finding a job on the open market.

A number of German towns and cities have for some time been pursuing similar strategies. In all, 2.5 million workers are in receipt of welfare from public funds, and it has been calculated that at least 700,000 of these would be available for work. Since the city of Lübeck discovered in 1996 that one-third of those claiming welfare never came back to the welfare office once they were offered a job, a number of local initiatives have been launched to help job-seekers.

In Dortmund, for instance, there are six council officials engaged solely in setting up contacts with prospective employers and placing as many long-term unemployed as possible. In a mere eight

months they negotiated 142 positions and saved the city 1.84
million marks. This initiative offers far more than the familiar
toing and froing between work-creation schemes and unemployment benefit. Bielefeld is another example of the successful
reintegration of the long-term unemployed, where more than
one period of further training has sometimes been necessary.
Hamburg and other cities have adopted the Dutch placement
scheme known as Maatwerk: here, for each unemployed man or
woman who has been more than six months in a job negotiated
by Maatwerk, the benefits office pays Maatwerk 4,000 marks.
According to the calculations of the Hamburg social security
office, 300 such placements will result in a saving of 3.8 million
marks in the city's welfare bill.

There is no automatic escape route out of the quagmire of
mass unemployment. It is all the more urgent, therefore, to
examine all the available options – what is feasible? what effect
would such-and-such measures have, and what would they cost?
The broader and more varied the spectrum of available options,
the greater the chances of a successful placement. The success
rate for the various schemes is put at between 10 and 55 per
cent. More, in this context, does not necessarily mean better, as
a comparison with other countries shows. In 1997 Germany spent
1.43 per cent of its gross domestic product on its employment
policies, with an unemployment rate of 10 per cent. In the
Netherlands it was only 1.37 per cent, with an unemployment
rate of 5.5 per cent, and in the UK a mere 0.46 per cent, where
the unemployment rate was 6.4 per cent. Sweden, on the other
hand, with an unemployment rate slightly higher than that in
Germany, invests a very much higher proportion of its GDP,
namely 2.25 per cent.

The crucial question is whether we can combine social security
and job-promotion in such a way as to produce more jobs and
more incentives to take up work. By accepting the alternative of
having a full-time job on the one hand and being unemployed on
the other, social security systems, given the fact of mass unemployment, are bound to fall into a trap. Instead, as they have
already done in Holland, we in Germany could make a considerable impact on the employment situation by means of a basic
security benefit financed from taxation and adapted to the needs
of the moment. In future only a maximum of 50 per cent of an
individual's own earnings would be set against the amount of the
basic security.

This proposal has a strong orientation towards economic and employment policy, since the basic security offers inducements to greater flexibility in the labour market, both on the supply and on the demand side. It encourages the opening up of new fields of activity and establishes conditions for the exercise of independence and personal initiative, thereby contributing to a better climate in industry and the labour market.

The German Institute for Economic Research and similar bodies assume that in Germany too the dynamism of low-paid and casual jobs could be extended to cover regular employment. A precondition would be a corresponding relief from wage-added costs, possibly through subsidizing welfare contributions for the lower-paid. All attempts to introduce a 'joint wage' seemed to have ended in tears. The volume of jobs in relatively unproductive service industries is limited on the demand side by high labour costs, and on the supply side by the greater attractiveness of welfare payments compared to low net incomes. For a person on welfare, taking on a poorly paid job or part-time employment is often less appealing a prospect than remaining dependent on state handouts. Many vacancies for service jobs with low productivity cannot be filled because it is not worth the worker's while. But only by a permanent expansion of jobs in the service industries providing for the domestic market can those of humbler expectations also have a chance to find their way to better-paid employment.

So within an agreed and legally defined framework a group of low-paid workers could be identified whose gross pay, paid by the employer, would be supplemented by a subsidy paid by the state. As the wage rose, so the subsidy would fall, and, like the other components of the wage, be subject to tax and national insurance contributions. It would be possible to introduce such a scheme in particular types of occupation and would, of course, have to be constantly supervised. As these subsidies would only be granted to those who paid tax and social security contributions, there would be a considerable incentive to legalize moonlighting and reduce the number of casual jobs. At the same time management and unions would be required to underwrite the resulting low-paid jobs.

Alternatively, the job effects and the incentive function of wage subsidization could be achieved by a reduction of welfare contributions at the lower end of the wage scale. Starting from a low base, at which the contributions of both employer and worker would be refunded in full, the concession would be withdrawn step by step and cease altogether at an upper level to be defined. The reduction of insurance contributions could be accommodated within the present wages structure. The gross wage paid by the employer would be brought down without the need for fresh negotiations over the rates for low-paid work. Again, this is a model that could be tried out in certain selected sectors or geographical areas.

Over the medium and short terms we need more political instruments in order to improve the transparency of the present system of welfare payments, facilitate the transition from unemployment to employment, create new fields of activity and encourage employers to take on less-qualified workers. Taking the social and political situation as it is, full employment can in future only offer a guarantee that no one will be permanently sidelined in the pursuit of his or her chosen career, or be for ever condemned to be unemployed or caught on the fringes of poverty in a poorly paid job.

The Challenge of the Pensions System

There is one more example of how the concept of normality is changing in Germany today, namely the provision of retirement pensions. New social constellations are emerging, such as the single parent family, usually female, who cannot pay sufficient contributions to guarantee a reasonable pension, or the steelworker thrown out of a job, or the white-collar worker, reasonably well off, who looks to banks and savings institutions to provide for retirement. The generation game needs new rules.

Increased life expectancy, changed family structures and dramatic changes in the labour markets are causing a crisis in the provision of retirement pensions. We have seen the crisis looming. Back in the mid-1980s discussions were being held on alternatives to the traditional pensions system in which politicians of all parties, economists, the social services and others involved in the problem took part. In the centre of those discussions stood the three basic principles that still apply today, principles still being discussed in ideological instead of realistic, pragmatic terms: a minimum basic pension plus supplements, the harmonization of pension schemes with the introduction of a minimum pension, and the extension of continuous supplementary assistance to provide general basic security for the elderly. Proposals for basic security financed out of taxation have been on the table since 1981.

In July 1997 the social research organization ZUMA reported as follows: 'In discussions on how to modernize the social security system the political parties have not yet been able to agree on any specific reform plans. Instead, the central components of the welfare system were one by one put up for discussion.' A poll later conducted by ZUMA revealed that two-thirds of those asked felt they were less than adequately insured. In contrast to the generations of the 'years of affluence', every third citizen now takes it for granted that from the age of 65 onwards he will be worse off than pensioners are today. This has an influence not only on people's sense of well-being, but also on social, political and economic systems. A quarter of those who consider themselves inadequately insured for their retirement say that they have no wish to vote in elections. People no longer know what they can depend on. The former Finance Minister Theo Waigel even threatened to tax life insurance.

All the initiatives tried have run up against institutionalized interests, and every new project has been interpreted as an attack on the 'contract between the generations'. But if we do nothing, and if, as has been forecast, by the year 2030 there will be one insurance payer for each pensioner, we shall stand accused of having betrayed the nation. The proportion of 65-year-olds in the population as a whole will by then have risen from 15.4 to 26.7 per cent, and there will be almost 20 million pensioners, compared with 12.5 million in 1996 – an increase of 60 per cent. If we had taken action 15 years ago, when all the facts were already on the table, today's debates over the length of the transition period needed during the changeover from a levy-financed system to a capital-based system, would be completely superfluous, and half the journey would already be behind us.

Thirty years ago the contribution rate for the state retirement pension stood at 14 per cent. By 1998 it was only prevented from going above the critical 20 per cent rate by an increase in value-added tax – and this too represented a delicate balancing act between system conformity and actually undermining the system. In all the tensions generated by talk of reform it went almost unheeded that in real terms pensions were declining. Among politicians it was a taboo subject, but many people saw it as a cynical ploy, and a large number of those who faithfully pay their contributions no longer believe that their money is safe in the hands of the state.

The Institute for Economics and Society in Bonn has calculated that a person who paid contributions between 1950 and 1994 would get back, on an average life expectancy, two marks for each mark paid in – a yield in real terms of 4.3 per cent per contribution year. But a person retiring in 2030 will receive only about 80 pfennigs for each mark contributed, unless the fund is substantially increased by monies from taxation. The precise figure may be open to question but the general trend is clear. Many see the state pension as only providing a basic degree of security, while at the same time private savings against retirement remain modest – one in every two has no money to invest in a private pension.

Given the present level of pensions, a typical wage-earner would need twenty-eight years of contributions to earn a pension exceeding the basic level of welfare. Contrary to what the image of the imaginary 'standard pensioner' implies, the typical pensioner in the former West Germany draws not 70 per cent but only 62 per cent of his or her average net income, because not even every second man, and only 5 per cent of women, reach the qualifying forty-five years of full-time employment. In 1996 the average pension earned by women in their own right after fifteen to twenty insurance years (the largest group) was 426,33 marks per month. Under conditions such as these the marriage market is more important for a woman's future than the labour market.

At the level of 64 per cent of average earnings, a typical worker would take thirty years to earn a pension that would exceed the level at which welfare became payable. In the case of the widows' pension, to reach the 60 per cent level would take the ridiculous figure of fifty-four years. These figures are not those which refer to the enjoyment of a comfortable, carefree life in retirement but only those which enable one to reach the level of welfare. It has been calculated that if the pension level were reduced to 60 per cent, almost one quarter of standard pensions for men and 95.5 per cent of those for women would fall below the welfare level. If one seriously wanted to cap pension contributions at 20 per cent, one would either have to raise the normal retirement age to 72 or set the level of pension at 56 per cent. But how could one convince the average worker of the virtue of contributing 20 per cent of his or her wages for a retirement pension, if at the end one worker in four is left with a pension that is no higher than welfare? The root of the problem of the generation conflict has long ceased to be that the burden of payment would be laid on the shoulders of our grandchildren – it is the present generation of wage-earners that is in the hot spot.

It is the labour market that exerts the farthest-reaching influence on our pensions system, dependent, as it is, on wages and contributions. Any blip in the employment figures shows itself immediately in rising claims and falling contributions. The German Ministry of Labour has calculated that between 1990 and 1995 the shortfall to the pension fund caused by registered unemployment amounted to 80 billion marks. The proportion of full-time jobs declines, the number of temporary and short-time jobs increases, and nothing suggests that we have any way out of the situation. The government was still happily assuming in 1997 that, contrary to all experience, the share of the overall employment potential that fell to regular full-time employees would increase from 66.5 to 75.9 per cent by the year 2030 – the sort of exaggerated forecast one used to associate with the command economies of socialist countries.

The facts make the situation clear. We can no longer take it for granted that the pension scheme alone, as it stands, will guarantee one's standard of living after the age of retirement – and people are aware of it. It is only due to a growing preparedness to make private provision for their retirement that poverty among the elderly has not become a widespread phenomenon. In other words, guaranteeing a comfortable old age has become a private concern. In 1992 83 per cent of married couples, 61 per cent of men living on their own and 75 per cent of widows have two, three and even four sources of income.

Thus, what the SPD proposes is in fact already in existence – a retirement scheme that draws on a number of different sources. But as things stand, the system is not transparent, and the potentialities are unequally distributed. A useful short-term measure would be the use of taxation monies as a supplementary source of income, but it could not be much more than a shot in the arm, and would amount in effect only to an increased subsidy from the federal government. And there are other arguments that have to be settled, such as how to treat the pension funds in the former East Germany. In hardly any other area of discussion does it emerge how defensive people have become about the entire

question of the future of retirement pensions. But most have come
to realize that it is neither fair nor rational to thrust the whole
burden on to those in regular full-time employment and exempt
other groups in the working population.

In a changed and changing world the status quo offers less
security than flexible reorganization. It is not discussions on theoretical systems that we need, but proposals for the solution of
concrete problems. The political parties must arrive at a consensus about what benefits the state is to provide, the level of such
benefits and the conditions of access to them, then turn that consensus into practical proposals for reform, with the aim of
producing a results-oriented social policy.

In 1997 Kurt Biedenkopf, Minister President of the *Land* of
Saxony, proposed a basic retirement pension funded from taxation. All those over 65 who had lived in Germany for at least
twenty-five years would receive 55 per cent of the average wage,
to which employees, employers and property-owners would con-
tribute, i.e. at present 1,540 marks a month, from which insurance contributions would be withheld. Anyone seeking a higher
figure than this would have to have recourse to private schemes.

Initial reaction to Biedenkopf's plan was not to touch it with
a barge pole. But not all the criticisms levelled against it were to
the point. One, for example, was that such a scheme was not
safe from the marauding hands of the Finance Minister, and
would become a fiscal football. But by 1998 it had already become
clear, from the decision of the previous conservative government
to lower the level of retirement pension, where the broader
political risks lay.

Another criticism was that the idea of a basic pension was at
odds with the principle of contributions. In this case we would
also have to submit our own system to a critical appraisal. Today
we tell workers in a small company that their life's work is worth
less than that of a worker in a Mercedes factory simply because
the latter earns more and has paid more in contributions. This
affects especially those who, having lost their job through no
fault of their own and lifted themselves up by their boot-straps
through a succession of low-paid and part-time jobs, now find
themselves let down for a second time. Does one, when calculating benefits, take account of the time women have spent on
bringing up a family? Is the principle of pension rights not guaranteed for those who can throughout their working life make

additional provision for their old age, so that they will have no need to fear that, when that time comes, they will find themselves under-insured?

Nor is the argument convincing that a basic pension would encourage people to take up moonlighting jobs. Indeed, it is the very combination of rising wages-added costs, falling real incomes and uncertain pension expectation that forces people into moonlighting and fraudulent self-employment. Moreover, thousands of genuinely self-employed already make their own decisions about how to provide for their retirement, without this apparently resulting in any significant under-insurance. Biedenkopf's plan may be too radical and not politically viable, but he asks the right questions.

In 1997 an SPD committee put forward a plan for a minimum pension which built as far as possible on elements of self-provision. Taking its lead from the Netherlands and Switzerland, the committee recommended the introduction of minimum contributions for all adults, combined with an additional sum dependent on income. A person for whom the minimum insurance contribution did not provide an adequate income on retirement would be cushioned by a basic pension calculated according to need. In addition to the minimum provision, an extra, privately funded sum would be needed – a stabilization of company pensions and increased scope for pension funds to diversify their investments.

One thing is clear. First, we need a secure pensions system which will satisfy the needs of three groups – the pensioners of today, those who will have a claim to a pension by virtue of having made lifelong contributions, and the younger generations. And secondly, we must allow people the freedom, according to their needs and the situation of the moment, to make their own provision for their retirement. A minimum pension must therefore be coupled with a substantial reduction, preferably by half, in contributions.

In the Netherlands a basic pension guaranteed by the state has had the result that people have become very much readier to embark on a flexible pattern of employment than in Germany. The basic pension for everyone amounts to 70 per cent of the legal minimum wage. Contrary to what is widely believed, this basic pension is not really funded from taxation: it is a general insurance scheme financed by contributions from the first of three stages of the national income tax rates (up to a taxable income of 45,960 guilders per year) – a uniform rate of 15.4 per cent. People who pay no income tax receive from the tax office a statement of their pensions contribution. Below a certain tax-free figure no contributions need to be made, while low incomes pay a lower rate. In contrast to the German practice, employers pay nothing towards contributions.

A person receiving the minimum wage or less is entirely dependent on this national insurance. For the majority of workers, however, the retirement pension will be topped up according to agreed rates. In this case employers and employees both pay into one of the state-approved pension funds. According to the sector and the size of the company, firms can choose between sector-linked funds and their own fund, make a contract with an approved insurance company or allow their employees to make their own insurance arrangements – in which case their pension claims can be transferred from one company to another if they change their job.

Sector funds have in the meantime become the biggest performers on the Dutch financial stage. The Dutch refer to the scheme as a whole as the 'cappuccino principle' – company pensions are the cream on the coffee of national insurance. Such is the flexibility of the scheme that more and more are making additional private provision for their pensions – the grated chocolate on top of the cream, so to speak. Switzerland has a similar model, in which long before retirement age one can withdraw one's collected savings in order, for example, to buy a new house as another way of providing for one's retirement.

The conclusion to be drawn from international discussions on the whole problem of pensions reform is that there is obviously a place in the provision of retirement pensions for both a levy and a capital-funded system. With these clear and logically argued projects in front of us, there is little room left for Norbert Blüm's backward-looking policies, which could not get away from an obsession with the funding problem and did not give the question of structural change a moment's thought.

According to the pollsters of the Emnid organization, 80 per cent of the gainfully employed population today would take provision for their retirement into their own hands. Indeed, 55 per cent already do so, with an average of 330 marks monthly per household. This produces a sum of 60 billion marks, one-fifth of the total paid into the state pension scheme. Life insurance is the most popular form of investment. One in three has taken out supplementary insurance or bought a house or an apartment to protect their retirement. Stocks and shares are also becoming increasingly popular, a development from which investment funds have greatly profited in the last few years. Insurance companies advise people to save 5 per cent of their gross income from the age of 40 onwards, in order to guarantee their comfort in retirement.

But a person with a family will find it hard to do this if insurance contributions rise, or even if they stay at their present level. Caught between falling real incomes and rising welfare contributions which no longer guarantee an assured future, many households find themselves unable to afford any further provision. Logically enough, over half of German households would prefer lower benefits from the state insurance scheme to higher rates of contributions. Any pensions reform worthy of the name must reduce the compulsory insurance contributions that these people have to pay.

It remains a cardinal principle that pensioners retain what they are entitled to. But we must start considering whether the present shaky system has not reached the point at which, in the interests of future generations, a radical overhaul has become essential. If we want to carry the people with us in introducing a modern, flexible social security scheme, we must have the courage to draw a line under the present system. By turning away from the problems, we only lead people to regard the mutual social security scheme that we have as a tiresome subject because of its lack of transparency and ultimate impermeability to reform. And as frustration grows, so more and more seek refuge in moonlighting and the grey economy.

What we now need is a guaranteed pension which provides a calculable minimum sum. To achieve this we only need to draw on the pragmatic proposals already on the table, and to compare them with the successful schemes that have been adopted by our neighbours. This guaranteed pension, financed through low contributions of less than 10 per cent on all sources of income, would be the equivalent of a levy but on a new basis. It would not be only the declining numbers of the regularly employed who had to fund this levy but all those in receipt of income, of whatever kind and from whatever source, each according to his abilities. At certain times the state would meet the contributions – for example, while the children were at school. One man, one pension – one woman, one pension.

Whether we achieve this through tax revenue, like the Netherlands, or by a special levy, as in Switzerland, is not our primary
concern. We must, however, ensure that the impression is not
given that pensions are being paid for out of general tax revenue.
Benefits and contributions must be clearly and intelligibly laid
out. A guaranteed retirement pension could then be conveni-
ently combined with basic social security.

We also need a second source of finance, secured on capital.
Contributions from employees and subsidies from employers,
which together must not be allowed to exceed the contribution
rate for the guaranteed pension, could from a certain salary level
upwards be paid into specific state-approved and state-supervised
funds. One would be able to see at any time how much was
in the account. Pension claims could be settled according to the
so-called splitting system between husband and wife, while
unmarried couples could opt for splitting if they wished. The
pension provided would have to be adaptable to changes in the
pensioner's circumstances, while the extension and encouragement of private plans, from life insurance policies to the purchase
of a purpose-built apartment for the elderly, would constitute
the third pillar of the system.

We urgently need an overhaul of company pensions, which
provide an important alternative system. There are two basic
possibilities. Companies can take out life insurance policies for
their employees, secured either on the firm's own pension fund
or a public insurance company. Alternatively, an employer can
make provision through pension reserves and take over the
management of the scheme as a direct commitment or put it in
the hands of a provident society.

Employers have long pressed for these alternatives to be supplemented from pension funds, as is done in the UK. Companies
would either pay guaranteed pensions or only guarantee specified
amounts, while over half the capital could be invested in shares.
Only the pensions would be taxed. The funds would have to be
kept separate from the company's profit and loss account. Funds
could also offer their own pension savings plans. The possibilities are legion. It would also be a sensible idea to encourage the
workers to participate more fully in wealth-creation schemes. A
precondition for this, however, would be the agreement of employers' and workers' organizations and a desire to see a thorough
reform of social policy as a whole.

There is a deep-seated suspicion in the ranks of many politicians, especially in the SPD, of capital-funded forms of retirement pension with a high degree of personal autonomy. One still hears people say that life insurance companies have more money than they know what to do with – though founders of new businesses and the self-employed have been scarcely aware of this excess capital. But the reality is that neither the Netherlands nor Switzerland has handed over the fate of the workers and their families to the sharks of the international money market. We are dealing with strictly regulated investments which spend little on publicity and administration, and of whose services consumer organizations and trade unions also make use. This is the basis on which the UK is restoring its ailing retirement pension system.

The American sociologist Norman Birnbaum is one who has suggested a pragmatic approach. If members of society are obliged to invest in the private sector, argues Birnbaum, they pay close attention to investment decisions that affect their personal interests. The billions of dollars that would flow into the private sector could be used to create social investment funds with which one could help to offset the inadequacies of our cultural and social infrastructure, inadequacies which do not automatically disappear with the growth of profits in the private sector.

In Germany any fundamental reform of the pensions system faces the problem of how to avoid a triple charge on the 25–45 age group during a transition period. In the first place this group would have to continue to shoulder responsibility for present-day pensions and for the outstanding claims; it would have to share in the provision of a basic pension funded from higher taxes, and finally it would have to build up funds to provide for its own retirement. But this generation is already burdened with rising taxes and higher insurance contributions. The welfare state is rapidly developing into an organization for the over-40s. Traditional risks are covered, albeit less and less adequately, but the new problems and opportunities that arise in the wake of different forms of employment, of transfers from training to employment and vice versa, and of new combinations of career and family – all this is not handled with sufficient flexibility.

A changeover is feasible, even though it becomes more difficult year by year to put into effect. A transition period of less than thirty years would be scarcely realistic. But as I have already said, if only we had made a start fifteen years ago, when the situation was already staring us in the face, we would now be half-way there. We need to bring the two sides together, those who gain from the old system and those who need to find new solutions – a trade-unionist in a permanent long-term job, for example, and a part-time telephonist, who in spite of raising a family is determined to pursue a career.

It is not without significance that alternative models attract the greatest approval among the under-40s. They are caught in a dilemma. On the one hand they see that their pension is not guaranteed and want to make additional provision for their retirement; on the other hand, increasing welfare contributions are preventing them from doing just that. They are public-spirited and responsible enough to be prepared to make concessions, provided they could be sure of being given more freedom of manoeuvre on the basis of a guaranteed pension and intelligently organized solutions to outstanding problems. They have no wish to give up their feeling of solidarity with the other generations because they know what this solidarity will ensure – clear obligations in return for a new sense of security.

This is the starting-point for a new social contract. It is the task of politicians to do everything in their power to improve the prospects of those whose role is the creation of the prosperity needed to finance retirement pensions and the entire welfare system. Therefore, to get rid of out-of-date features of our education system, to make our universities centres for training founders of new businesses and to promote the cause of innovation, are all as vital for the future of retirement pensions as is the question of the average level of those pensions or the age at which they should become payable.

Postscript
Gerhard Schröder

The result of the German general election in 1998 was a vote of confidence in the country's future. The New Centre has given its support to the Social Democrats. Many self-employed and those who create the real wealth of our society, men and women alike, have withdrawn their support from the Christian Democrats. The SPD offers them the opportunity to forge a new social contract, to form new alliances.

But I also have in mind the many smaller alliances between those who have been driven apart by the policies of the past sixteen years and who have a shared interest in the modernization of society and the economy – people such as members of works councils and management boards who are up to their necks in everyday problems and who have long since realized that only in partnership can they remain competitive, yet see themselves let down both by captains of industry and by politicians. We need fresh coalitions among those who are looking for chances to show their initiative and need to be supported but who, through a series of misdirected policies, have found their freedom of movement curtailed rather than encouraged.

As we stand at the threshold of a new millennium, the major questions confronting us appear to be solved. Germany is politically reunited, albeit socially still divided, and European integration has acquired a new dimension. Helmut Kohl played an historic role in this and he merits our respect. But we are now confronting new problems, above all the harmonization of the economy and the labour market – the dynamization of the growth in which everyone must be allowed to share.

The reunification of Germany has put the country under severe strain. The decisive factor in the election was anxiety over the high rate of unemployment, coupled with the confidence that it would be the SPD that would tackle it most effectively. As to foreign policy, on the other hand, I hold to my promise to preserve continuity. Particularly in East Germany the voters had come to realize that innovation and social justice are two sides of the same coin. The problems that this book so clearly and openly identifies will not be easily solved. There is a pressing need for modernization. Our first and foremost task is to restore a consensus over ends and means as we set out to modernize the welfare state and the corporate sector, the federal system and the interventions of the state itself. People are looking for well-conceived, workable policies which face up to concrete issues. Hence my pledge, not that we shall do everything differently but that we shall do many things better.

The touchstone of the government's actions will be their effectiveness in the field of employment. We shall put every instrument to the acid test of whether it guarantees the jobs that are already there and creates new ones. That is the first of the five principles that govern our policies. We must tap the competitive energies and the creative power of our people. The state's duty is to help, not to hinder.

Our second principle is to employ a radical pragmatism in order to regain our facility for political action. One example of this would be the introduction of a modern employment policy providing for more part-time working, coupled with an education and further training drive designed to lead to higher qualifications. Also part of this initiative is a modernization of society and the economy which would enable women, in particular, to continue in active employment if they so desired. And there would also be a reform of the taxation system to encourage companies to invest in jobs. These are just a few examples – this book contains many more. We must part company with old ideas and concepts, such as the model of a patronizing, bureaucratic welfare state, or conventional assumptions about life, work and the economy which no longer have their roots in reality.

Our third principle requires us to evolve new policies to exploit the opportunities offered by globalization. During the chancellorship of Helmut Schmidt the concept of the 'German Model' was put forward, in which the Social Democrats set out to combine modernity with social responsibility, and thereby to make themselves the party of the future. The same plan occupies our minds today, though this time it will embrace the whole of Germany.

Principle four: whatever projects we propose must be capable of being checked for their effectiveness. The experience of the Netherlands teaches us that not all laws have to be made for eternity.

And, finally, we shall seek to co-operate with all sections of society, irrespective of formal position or responsibility. This book gives many examples of where successful policies have been carried through on such a basis.

The existence of a federal Alliance for Training and Labour cannot be allowed to blur the distinction between the responsibilities of the state and those of organized private interests, nor can we expect to find any quick and painless remedies. The federal government, however, led by the SPD, will join with employers and unions in searching for ways, through agreed policies, a modernization of the social security system and a balanced taxation policy, of improving conditions for the creation of new jobs – ways that reinforce, through reforms, the opportunities inherent in a diversified and flexible redistribution of labour.

Urgent measures are needed to deal with youth unemployment and long-term unemployment, to reduce employers' wage-added costs, to encourage the extension of flexible working hours and above all to bring about an improvement in the employment situation in East Germany. The new government will urge employers and unions to come to speedy agreements on these matters, while the state itself pursues measures against moonlighting and the grey economy, encourages the extension of part-time working and seeks a long-term improvement in the conditions of training. Without an agreed diagnosis of the problems there can be no effective cure. Consensus and co-operation must be the dominant characteristic of the new Berlin Republic.

In recent years politicians have played too much on people's fears and anxieties. Those days have gone. Bodo Hombach's book points forward to a new era in which innovation and social justice, the economy and the labour market can live side-by-side, and in which we can invest our technological advances in the preservation of the environment. Germany is seeking to join in the upswing that is sweeping through the whole of Europe, where our EU partners have drawn fresh strength from fresh ideas. So it is in

the United Kingdom, in France, in the Netherlands – wherever
social democrats have introduced and carried through reforms.
And so it will be in Germany too. Europe has had to wait long
enough for us to join it. Europe is much more than just the euro
– it is the greatest reform project in the whole of history, a
gigantic endeavour for us, as nation-states, to learn from one
another within a single community.

Tony Blair urged his friends to 'think the unthinkable' – pragmatism with visions, visions of a politics beyond left and right. This
is the spirit behind my challenge: 'We cannot afford the luxury
of procrastination.' In a constantly changing society and fluctuating
economic conditions there are no longer any commandments
carved in stone. We must always keep one step ahead and think
beyond the needs of the moment. Bodo Hombach's analyses of
the politically most important questions lay down an ideological
challenge. That practical problems do not always lead to the same
solutions as those prescribed in party political programmes, and
that facts are capable of being interpreted in other ways than
hitherto – this I welcome as an opportunity, not fear as a risk.

Bodo Hombach wants to put an end to the sense of stagnation
that afflicts politics and society. It is high time that the package
of measures universally recognized as essential was put into practice. He is less concerned, however, with issuing detailed pre-
scriptions than with how we can arrive at a new consensus for
the necessary reforms without delay. He knows that it is sometimes only by giving offence that one can get things moving. An
independent mind, he showed long ago that he is a loyal supporter of the SPD and its policies, and I welcome the frankness
with which he puts out new ideas with which I myself do not
necessarily agree in every detail. But we share the vision of a
proactive state that will set out to change society.

Not long ago I caused indignation by maintaining that there
was no longer a left-wing economic policy and a right-wing economic policy, but only a right policy or a wrong policy. This
book proceeds from the premise that there is consensus on this
today in Europe and beyond, and I am of the view that what I
said at that time in reference to economic policy can be applied
equally to other areas of politics. Hombach is right to set a
political benchmark. In this way Europe's social democrats will
come to learn from each other, complement each other and
stimulate each other.

Europe: The Third Way / Die Neue Mitte

Tony Blair and Gerhard Schröder

Introduction

Social democrats are in government in almost all the countries of the Union. Social democracy has found new acceptance – but only because, while retaining its traditional values, it has begun in a credible way to renew its ideas and modernize its programmes. It has also found new acceptance because it stands not only for social justice but also for economic dynamism and the unleashing of creativity and innovation.

The trademark of this approach is the New Centre in Germany and the Third Way in the United Kingdom. Other social democrats choose other terms that suit their own national cultures. But though the language and the institutions may differ, the motivation is everywhere the same. Most people have long since abandoned the world-view represented by the dogmas of left and right. Social democrats must be able to speak to those people.

Fairness and social justice, liberty and equality of opportunity, solidarity and responsibility to others – these values are timeless. Social democracy will never sacrifice them. To make these values relevant to today's world requires realistic and forward-looking policies capable of meeting the challenges of the twenty-first century. Modernization is about adapting to conditions that have objectively changed, and not reacting to polls.

Similarly, we need to apply our politics within a new economic framework, modernized for today, where government does all it can to support enterprise but never believes it is a substitute for enterprise. The essential function of markets must be complemented and improved by political action, not hampered by it. We support a market economy, not a market society.

We share a common destiny within the European Union. We face the same challenges – to promote employment and prosperity, to offer every individual the opportunity to fulfil their unique potential, to combat social exclusion and poverty, to reconcile material progress with environmental sustainability and our responsibility to future generations, to tackle common problems that threaten the cohesion of society such as crime and drugs, and to make Europe a more effective force for good in the world.

We need to strengthen our policies by benchmarking our experiences in Britain and Germany, but also with like-minded counterparts in Europe and the rest of the world. We must learn from each other and measure our own performance against best practice and experience in other countries. With this appeal, we invite other European social democratic governments who share our modernizing aims to join us in this enterprise.

I.

Learning from experience

Although both parties can be proud of our historic achievements, today we must develop realistic and feasible answers to new challenges confronting our societies and economies. This requires adherence to our values but also a willingness to change our old approaches and traditional policy instruments. In the past:

- The promotion of social justice was sometimes confused with the imposition of equality of outcome. The result was a neglect of the importance of rewarding effort and responsibility, and the association of social democracy with conformity and mediocrity rather than the celebration of creativity, diversity and excellence. Work was burdened with ever higher costs.
- The means of achieving social justice became identified with ever higher levels of public spending regardless of what they achieved or the impact of the taxes required to fund it on competitiveness, employment and living standards. Decent public services are a vital concern for social democrats, but social conscience cannot be measured by the level of public expenditure. The real test for society is how effectively this expenditure is used and how much it enables people to help themselves.
- The belief that the state should address damaging market failures all too often led to a disproportionate expansion of the government's reach and the bureaucracy that went with it. The balance between the individual and the collective was distorted. Values that are important to citizens, such as

personal achievement and success, entrepreneurial spirit, individual responsibility and community spirit, were too often subordinated to universal social safeguards.

- Too often rights were elevated above responsibilities, but the responsibility of the individual to his or her family, neighbourhood and society cannot be off-loaded on to the state. If the concept of mutual obligation is forgotten, this results in a decline in community spirit, lack of responsibility towards neighbours, rising crime and vandalism, and a legal system that cannot cope.
- The ability of national governments to fine-tune the economy in order to secure growth and jobs has been exaggerated. The importance of individual and business enterprise to the creation of wealth has been undervalued. The weaknesses of markets have been overstated and their strengths underestimated.

II.

New programmes for changed realities

Ideas of what is 'left-wing' should never become an ideological straitjacket.

The politics of the New Centre and Third Way is about addressing the concerns of people who live and cope with societies undergoing rapid change – both winners and losers. In this newly emerging world people want politicians who approach issues without ideological preconceptions and who, applying their values and principles, search for practical solutions to their problems through honest well-constructed and pragmatic policies. Voters who in their daily lives have to display initiative and adaptability in the face of economic and social change expect the same from their governments and their politicians.

- In a world of ever more rapid globalization and scientific changes we need to create the conditions in which existing businesses can prosper and adapt, and new businesses can be set up and grow.
- New technologies radically change the nature of work and internationalize the organization of production. With one hand they de-skill and make some businesses obsolete, with another they create new business and vocational opportunities. The most important task of modernization is to invest in human capital: to make the individual and businesses fit for the know-ledge-based economy of the future.
- Having the same job for life is a thing of the past. Social democrats must accommodate the growing demands for

flexibility – and at the same time maintain minimum social standards, help families to cope with change and open up fresh opportunities for those who are unable to keep pace.

- We face an increasing challenge in reconciling environmental responsibility towards future generations with material progress for society at large. We must marry environmental responsibility with a modern market-based approach. In environmental protection, the most modern technologies consume fewer resources, open up new markets and create new jobs.
- Public expenditure as a proportion of national income has more or less reached the limits of acceptability. Constraints on 'tax and spend' force radical modernization of the public sector and reform of public services to achieve better value for money. The public sector must actually serve the citizen: we do not hesitate to promote the concepts of efficiency, competition and high performance.
- Social security systems need to adapt to changes in life expectancy, family structures and the role of women. Social democrats need to find ways of combating the ever more pressing problems of crime, social disintegration and drug abuse. We need to take the lead in shaping a society with equal rights for women and men.
- Crime is a vital political issue for modern social democrats. We consider safety on the street to be a civil right. A policy to make cities worth living in fosters community spirit, creates new jobs and makes residential areas safer.
- Poverty remains a central concern, especially among families with children. We need specific measures for those who are most threatened by marginalization and social exclusion.

This also requires a modern approach to government:

- The state should not row, but steer: not so much control, as challenge. Solutions to problems must be joined up.
- Within the public sector bureaucracy at all levels must be reduced, performance targets and objectives formulated, the quality of public services rigorously monitored, and bad performance rooted out.
- Modern social democrats solve problems where they can best be solved. Some problems can now only be tackled at European level: others, such as the recent financial crises, require

increased international co-operation. But, as a general principle, power should be devolved to the lowest possible level.

For the new politics to succeed, it must promote a go-ahead mentality and a new entrepreneurial spirit at all levels of society. That requires:

- a competent and well-trained workforce eager and ready to take on new responsibilities;
- a social security system that opens up new opportunities and encourages initiative, creativity and readiness to take on new challenges;
- a positive climate for entrepreneurial independence and initiative. Small businesses must become easier to set up and better able to survive;
- we want a society which celebrates successful entrepreneurs just as it does artists and footballers – and which values creativity in all spheres of life.

Our countries have different traditions in dealings between state, industry, trade unions and social groups, but we share a conviction that traditional conflicts at the workplace must be overcome. This, above all, means rekindling a spirit of community and solidarity, strengthening partnership and dialogue between all groups in society and developing a new consensus for change and reform. We want all groups in society to share our joint commitment to the new directions set out in this Declaration.

Immediately upon taking office, the new Social Democratic government in Germany gathered the top representatives of the political sector, the business community and the unions around the table to forge an Alliance for Jobs, Training and Competitiveness.

- We want to see real partnership at work, with employees having the opportunity of sharing the rewards of success with employers.
- We support modern trade unions protecting individuals against arbitrary behaviour, and working in co-operation with employers to manage change and create long-term prosperity.
- In Europe – under the umbrella of a European employment pact – we will strive to pursue an ongoing dialogue with the social partners that supports, not hinders, necessary economic change.

III.

A new supply-side agenda for the left

The task facing Europe is to meet the challenge of the global economy while maintaining social cohesion in the face of real and perceived uncertainty. Rising employment and expanding job opportunities are the best guarantee of a cohesive society.

The past two decades of neo-liberal laissez-faire are over. In its place, however, there must not be a renaissance of 1970s-style reliance on deficit spending and heavy-handed state intervention. Such an approach now points in the wrong direction.

Our national economies and global economic relationships have undergone profound change. New conditions and new realities call for a re-evaluation of old ideas and the development of new concepts.

In much of Europe unemployment is far too high – and a high proportion of it is structural. To address this challenge, Europe's social democrats must together formulate and implement a new supply-side agenda for the left.

Our aim is to modernize the welfare state, not dismantle it: to embark on new ways of expressing solidarity and responsibility to others without basing the motivation for economic activity on pure undiluted self-interest.

The main elements of this approach are as follows:

A robust and competitive market framework

Product market competition and open trade is essential to stimulate productivity and growth. For that reason a framework that allows market forces to work properly is essential to economic success and a precondition of a more successful employment policy.

- The EU should continue to act as a resolute force for liberalization of world trade.
- The EU should build on the achievements of the single market to strengthen an economic framework conducive to productivity growth.

A tax policy to promote sustainable growth

In the past social democrats became identified with high taxes, especially on business. Modern social democrats recognize that in the right circumstances, tax reform and tax cuts can play a critical part in meeting their wider social objectives.

For instance, corporate tax cuts raise profitability and strengthen the incentives to invest. Higher investment expands economic activity and increases productive potential. It helps create a virtuous circle of growth increasing the resources available for public spending on social purposes.

- The taxation of companies should be simplified and corporation tax rates cut, as they have been by New Labour in the UK and are planned by the federal government in Germany.
- To ensure work pays and to improve the fairness of the tax system, the tax burden borne by working families and workers should be alleviated, as begun in Germany (through the Tax Relief Act) – and the introduction of lower starting rates of income tax and the working families tax credit in Britain.
- The willingness and ability of enterprises – especially small and medium-sized enterprises – to invest should be enhanced, as intended by the Social Democratic government in Germany through the reform of the taxes on businesses and as shown by New Labour's reform of capital gains and business taxes in Britain.
- Overall, the taxation of hard work and enterprise should be reduced. The burden of taxation should be rebalanced, for example towards environmental 'bads'. Germany, the UK and other European countries governed by social democrats will lead the way in this regard.
- At EU level, tax policy should support tough action to combat unfair competition and fight tax evasion. This requires enhanced

co-operation, not uniformity. We will not support measures leading to a higher tax burden and jeopardizing competitiveness and jobs in the EU.

Demand- and supply-side policies go together – they are not alternatives

In the past social democrats often gave the impression that the objectives of growth and high unemployment would be achieved by successful demand management alone. Modern social democrats recognize that supply-side policies have a central and complementary role to play.

In today's world most policy decisions have an impact on both supply- and demand-side conditions.

- Successful Welfare to Work programmes raise incomes for those previously out of work as well as improve the supply of labour available to employers.
- Modern economic policy aims to increase the after-tax income of workers and at the same time decrease the costs of labour to the employer. The reduction of non-wage labour costs through structural reform of social security systems and a more employment-friendly tax and contribution structure that looks to the future is therefore of particular importance.

The aim of social democratic policy is to overcome the apparent contradiction between demand- and supply-side policies in favour of a fruitful combination of microeconomic flexibility and macroeconomic stability.

To achieve higher growth and more jobs in today's world, economies must be adaptable: flexible markets are a modern social democratic aim.

Macroeconomic policy still has a vital purpose: to set the conditions for stable growth and avoid boom and bust. But social democrats must recognize that getting the macroeconomics right is not sufficient to stimulate higher growth and more jobs. Changes in interest rates or tax policy will not lead to increased investment and employment unless the supply side of the economy is adaptable enough to respond. To make the European economy more dynamic, we also need to make it more flexible.

- Companies must have room for manoeuvre to take advantage of improved economic conditions and seize new opportunities: they must not be gagged by rules and regulations.
- Product, capital and labour markets must all be flexible: we must not combine rigidity in one part of the economic system with openness and dynamism in the rest.

Adaptability and flexibility are at an increasing premium in the knowledge-based service economy of the future

Our economies are in transition – from industrial production to the knowledge-based service economy of the future. Social democrats must seize the opportunity of this radical economic change. It offers Europe a chance to catch up with the United States. It offers millions of our people the chance to find new jobs, learn new skills, pursue new careers, set up and expand new businesses – in summary, to realize their hopes of a better future.

But social democrats have to recognize that the basic requirements for economic success have changed. Services cannot be kept in stock: customers use them as and when they are needed – at many different times of day, outside what people think of as normal working hours. The rapid advance of the information age, especially the huge potential of electronic commerce, promises to change radically the way we shop, the way we learn, the way we communicate and the way we relax. Rigidity and over-regulation hamper our success in the knowledge-based service economy of the future. They will hold back the potential of innovation to generate new growth and more jobs. We need to become more flexible, not less.

An active government, in a newly conceived role, has a key role to play in economic development

Modern social democrats are not laissez-faire neo-liberals. Flexible markets must be combined with a newly defined role for an active state. The top priority must be investment in human and social capital.

If high employment is to be achieved and sustained, employees must react to shifting demands. Our economies suffer from a considerable discrepancy between the number of job vacancies that need to be filled (for example in the field of information and communication technology) and the number of suitably qualified applicants.

That means education must not be a 'one-off' opportunity: lifetime access to education and training and lifelong utilization of their opportunities represent the most important security available in the modern world. Therefore, governments have a responsibility to put in place a framework that enables individuals to enhance their qualifications and to fulfil their potential. This must now be a top social democratic priority.

- Standards at all levels of schooling and for all abilities of pupils must be raised. Where there are problems of literacy and numeracy these must be addressed, otherwise we condemn unskilled individuals to lives of low pay, insecurity and unemployment.
- We want all young people to have the opportunity to gain entry into the world of work by means of qualified vocational training. Together with local employers, trade unions and others, we must ensure that sufficient education and training opportunities are available to meet the requirements of the local labour market. In Germany, the political sector is supporting this endeavour with an immediate action programme for jobs and training that will enable 100,000 young people to find a new job or training place or to obtain qualifications. In Britain the Welfare to Work programme has already enabled 95,000 young people to find work.
- We need to reform post-school education and raise its quality, at the same time modernizing education and training programmes so as to promote adaptability and employability in later life. Government has a particular role in providing incentives for individuals to save in order to meet the costs of lifelong learning – and in widening access through the promotion of distance learning.
- We should ensure that training plays a significant role in our active labour market policies for the unemployed and workless households.

A modern and efficient public infrastructure including a strong scientific base is also an essential feature of a job-generating economy. It is important to ensure that the composition of public expenditure is being directed at activities most beneficial to growth and fostering necessary structural change.

*Modern social democrats should be champions of small
and medium-sized enterprise*

The development of prosperous small and medium-sized businesses has to be a top priority for modern social democrats. Here
lies the biggest potential for new growth and jobs in the knowledge-based society of the future.

People in many different walks of life are looking for the
opportunity to become entrepreneurs – long-standing as well as
newly self-employed people, lawyers, computer experts, medical
doctors, craftsmen, business consultants, people active in culture
and sport. These individuals must have scope to develop economic
initiative and create new business ideas. They must be encouraged to take risks. The burdens on them must be lightened. Their
markets and their ambitions must not be hindered by borders.

- Europe's capital markets should be opened up so that growing firms and entrepreneurs can have ready access to finance.
  We intend to work together to ensure that growing high-tech
  firms enjoy the same access to the capital markets as their US
  rivals.
- We should make it easy for individuals to set up businesses
  and for new companies to grow by lightening administrative
  burdens, exempting small businesses from onerous regulations
  and widening access to finance. We should make it easier for
  small businesses in particular to take on new staff: that means
  lowering the burden of regulation and non-wage labour costs.
- The links between business and the science base should be
  strengthened to ensure more entrepreneurial 'spin-offs' from
  research and the promotion of 'clusters' of new high-tech
  industries.

*Sound public finance should be a badge of pride for
social democrats*

In the past, social democrats have all too often been associated
with the view that the best way to promote employment and
growth is to increase government borrowing in order to finance
higher government spending. We do not rule out government deficits
– during a cyclical downturn it makes sense to let the automatic
stabilizers work. And borrowing to finance higher government

investment, in strict accordance with the Golden Rule, can play a key role in strengthening the supply side of the economy.

However, deficit spending cannot be used to overcome structural weaknesses in the economy that are a barrier to faster growth and higher employment. Social democrats also must not tolerate excessive levels of public sector debt. Increased indebtedness represents an unfair burden on future generations. It could have unwelcome redistributive effects. Above all, money spent on servicing high public sector debt is not available to be spent on other priorities, including increased investment in education, training or the transport infrastructure.

From the standpoint of a supply-side policy of the left, it is essential that high levels of government borrowing decrease and not increase.

IV.

An active labour market policy for the left

The state must become an active agent for employment, not merely the passive recipient of the casualties of economic failure.

People who have never had experience of work or who have been out of work for long periods lose the skills necessary to compete in the labour market. Prolonged unemployment also damages individual life chances in other ways and makes it more difficult for individuals to participate fully in society.

A welfare system that puts limits on an individual's ability to find a job must be reformed.

Modern social democrats want to transform the safety net of entitlements into a springboard to personal responsibility.

For our societies, the imperatives of social justice are more than the distribution of cash transfers. Our objective is the widening of equality of opportunity, regardless of race, age or disability, to fight social exclusion and ensure equality between men and women.

People rightly demand high-quality public services and solidarity for all who need help – but also fairness towards those who pay for it. All social policy instruments must improve life chances, encourage self-help and promote personal responsibility.

With this aim in mind, the health care system and the system for ensuring financial security in old age are being thoroughly modernized in Germany by adapting both to the changes in life expectancy and changing lifelong patterns of employment, without sacrificing the principle of solidarity. The same thinking applies to the introduction of stakeholder pensions and the reform of disability benefits in Britain.

Periods of unemployment in an economy without jobs for life must become an opportunity to attain qualifications and foster personal development. Part-time work and low-paid work are better than no work because they ease the transition from unemployment to jobs.

New policies to offer unemployed people jobs and training are a social democratic priority – but we also expect everyone to take up the opportunity offered.

But providing people with the skills and abilities to enter the workforce is not enough. The tax and benefits systems need to make sure it is in people's interests to work. A streamlined and modernized tax and benefits system is a significant component of the left's active supply-side labour market policy. We must:

• Make work pay for individuals and families. The biggest part of the income must remain in the pockets of those who worked for it.

• Encourage employers to offer 'entry' jobs to the labour market by lowering the burden of tax and social security contributions on low-paid jobs. We must explore the scope to lower the burden of non-wage labour costs by environmental taxes.

• Introduce targeted programmes for the long-term unemployed and other disadvantaged groups to give them the opportunity to reintegrate into the labour market on the principle of rights and responsibilities going together.

• Assess all benefit recipients, including people of working age in the receipt of disability benefits, for their potential to earn, and reform state employment services to assist those capable of work to find appropriate work.

• Support enterprise and setting up an own business as a viable route out of unemployment. Such decisions contain considerable risks for those who dare to make such a step. We must support those people by managing these risks.

The left's supply-side agenda will hasten structural change. But it will also make that change easier to live with and manage.

Adapting to change is never easy and the speed of change appears faster than ever before, not least under the impact of new technologies. Change inevitably destroys some jobs, but it creates others.

However, there can be lags between job losses in one sector and the creation of new jobs elsewhere. Whatever the longer-term benefits for economies and living standards, particular industries and communities can experience the costs before the gains. Hence we must focus our efforts on easing localized problems of transition. The dislocating effects of change will be greater the longer they are resisted, but it is no good pretending that they can be wished away.

Adjustment will be the easier, the more labour and product markets are working properly. Barriers to employment in relatively low-productivity sectors need to be lowered if employees displaced by the productivity gains that are an inherent feature of structural change are to find jobs elsewhere. The labour market needs a low-wage sector in order to make low-skill jobs available. The tax and benefits system can replenish low incomes from employment and at the same time save on support payments for the unemployed.

V.
Political benchmarking in Europe

The challenge is the definition and implementation of a new social democratic politics in Europe. We do not advocate a single European model, still less the transformation of the European Union into a superstate. We are pro-Europe and pro-reform in Europe. People will support further steps towards integration where there is real value-added and they can be clearly justified – such as action to combat crime and destruction of the environment as well as the promotion of common goals in social and employment policy. But at the same time Europe urgently needs reform – more efficient and transparent institutions, reform of outdated policies and decisive action against waste and fraud.

We are presenting our ideas as an outline, not a finalized programme. The politics of the New Centre and the Third Way is already a reality in many city councils, in reformed national policies, in European co-operation and in new international initiatives.

To this end the German and British governments have decided to embed their existing arrangements for exchanging views on policy development in a broader approach. We propose to do this in three ways:

- First, there will be a series of ministerial meetings, supported by frequent contacts among their close staff.
- We will seek discussion with political leaders in other European countries who wish to take forward with us modernizing ideas for social democracy in their respective national contexts. We will start on this now.

- We will establish a network of experts, far-sighted thinkers, political fora and discussion meetings. We will thereby deepen and continually further develop the concept of the New Centre and the Third Way. This is the priority for us.

The aim of this declaration is to give impetus to modernization. We invite all social democrats in Europe not to let this historic opportunity for renewal pass by. The diversity of our ideas is our greatest asset for the future. Our societies expect us to knit together our diverse experiences in a new coherent programme.

Let us together build social democracy's success for the new century. Let the politics of the Third Way and the Neue Mitte be Europe's new hope.

Index